The Old Testament and Theology

The Old Testament and Theology

by
G. Ernest Wright

1817

HARPER & ROW, PUBLISHERS
New York, Evanston, and London

FIRST EDITION

LIBRARY OF CONGRESS CATALOG CARD NUMBER: 69-17022

To Joseph Haroutunian
long my mentor in theology,
trusted friend
and unusual critic

Contents

Introduction		9
1	*Theology and Christomonism*	13
2	*Revelation and Theology*	39
3	*God the Creator*	70
4	*God the Lord*	97
5	*God the Warrior*	121
6	*Language, Symbol and Faith*	151
7	*The Canon as Theological Problem*	166
Index		187

Introduction

THE PURPOSE of this volume is the attempt to say what consequences follow for theology when one takes the Old Testament seriously: not seriously as solely a historical document of importance only as background for later movements, but vitally as canonical and of serious moment for present faith and life. Limitations of space mean that only a few central issues can be touched upon. Yet each of these is considered a basic one, and often controversial because it runs counter to much that is being done as theology by "younger" theologians at the present time.

The last three decades have been an exciting era for teachers of the Old Testament, because the problem of faith in the often dreadful flux of human history has struck a current human concern at a time when Old Testament scholarship was in the midst of a drastic reassessment of its procedures and goals. Yet as we enter the last third of the twentieth century we find our theological positions, partially drawn from the "fresh" discovery of the Old Testament, often challenged or ignored. It may be of value, therefore, to think about certain fundamentals in the current context of discussion, and to ask how a case can be made for them and what is implied when one does so.

First of all, the Christian Old Testament scholar, if he is to think about the theological importance of his material at all, must reject certain varieties of Christocentricity which dissolve theology into Christology, leaving one with nothing to say about the independence of God. In such theologies God has so surrendered himself in the Christ-event that when one has said all things needful about it, he understands that little more need be said about God. This results in what H. Richard Niebuhr has called a Christian "henotheism"

9

which substitutes Christ for God.[1] At a time when specific content within the term "God" is for many a great difficulty, forms of Christomonism appear increasingly like a "superstition" which is not necessarily a help for faith.

If one can agree in general thus far (through Chap. 1!), then the Old Testament scholar can begin to speak. For example, what has the centrality of the historical narrative form of revelation to say concerning the nature of theology as a discipline (Chap. 2)? The different efforts currently available as Old Testament theology illustrate the problem, for each has its own conception of the nature of theology which is then employed to unlock the Bible for use in our time. What does it mean to "do" theology when "systematic" theology must make do without systems and when one can no longer simply say that theology is "the rational content of faith"?

Chapters 3—5 form the center of the book. Here an attempt is made to raise certain issues without which the Bible would not be what it is amidst the variety of religious forms in the world. The proposition is that what is basically Biblical is a special political understanding of the universe. This means that life is a responsible vocation under the Lord of time and event. It also means that one's language takes form around particular political forms of the world which are sublimated for theological use. Three conceptions are examined as to how they are Biblically understood, how they bear on the political issue, and how they are still meaningful. These are God the Creator, Lord, and Warrior.

In Chapter 6 the question is faced as to how one can live with such conceptions, basic though they are to the Bible. Here Bultmann's program of demythologizing is rejected (without argument) in favor of Calvin's principle of accommodation and Tillich's interpretation of the religious symbol. Calvin and Tillich are often seen to be diametrically opposite each other at this point, but the chapter argues that this is not necessarily the case. Finally, it is noted that a presupposition of the whole book is that there is such a thing as a canon of Scripture which is still theologically meaning-

[1] Quoted in context in Chap. 1, n. 16.

ful. Chapter 7 attempts to state why this is a theological problem
in our time and one way in which it may be treated.

In 1949–1950 I wrote *God Who Acts: Biblical Theology as
Recital* with all the enthusiasm of fresh discovery and with the ex-
aggeration which came from personal reaction against the view of
theology in which I had been reared.[2] It is my hope that this
volume carries the discussion forward far beyond the position of
that book, while still accepting its general argument as important
prolegomena to the further steps that must be taken in the light of
more recent research, sober reflection, and the new era in which
we now live.

The chapters to follow are an expanded version of the Sprunt
Lectures, given at Union Theological Seminary in Richmond,
Virginia, during the first week in March, 1968. My warm thanks
are here expressed to President Fred R. Stair, Jr. and to the members of the faculty for extending me the invitation and for their
hospitality while I was among them. A special word of gratitude
must also be expressed to Thomas D. Newman and Conrad
l'Heureux of the American Schools of Oriental Research and of
the Harvard Graduate School of Arts and Sciences respectively for
assistance beyond the call of duty. The latter prepared the index.

Scripture translations are my own except where noted.

G. ERNEST WRIGHT

*Lexington, Massachusetts
April, 1969*

[2] Published in 1952 as *Studies in Biblical Theology*, No. 8 (London:
SCM Press, and Naperville, Ill.: Alec R. Allenson; 7th impression,
1964).

1

Theology and Christomonism

THE FIRST suggestion that an Old Testament scholar must make to the theologian is this: Any form of theology unable to deal positively with the Old Testament as a dynamic part of western civilization—and its Judeo-Christian heritage—must come in for serious critical scrutiny. In this first chapter, certain Christocentric theologies will be the subject of specific protest (1) because of the severe limitations they place on the believer's perspective and (2) because of the sore problems they present to faith at a time when all faith, whether in man or in God, is in difficulty.

Every Christian is by definition Christ-centered in some sense. Yet when all that is true and good and important for us in the Bible is restricted to the life and teachings of Jesus, the Christian finds himself severely limited in facing the issues of meaning and value in current life and history.

For one thing, Christianity has always claimed to be trinitarian, no matter how difficult it has been to formulate what that means. Yet one basic meaning must surely involve the Christian's attempt to summarize God's relation to the world as the Bible presents it. It is no simple relation; it is complex. Trinity cannot refer in this first instance to the *being* of God but rather to the ways God has related himself to our fathers and to us. No unitarianism of the Second Person of the Trinity (in Elton Trueblood's phrase) is adequate for the complexity of historical experience as the Bible interprets it.

Then again, Messianic or Christological language in the Bible refers primarily to Christ's relation to God. For example, in Isaiah 9:6 the name of the Messiah of Israel is given as "Wonderful Counselor" (that is, a Marvel in the Role of Adviser), "Mighty

13

God" (the Divine Warrior), "Everlasting Father" (always or eternally a Father in relation to his people), "Prince of Peace" (the official whose responsibility is peace). Since it was common in antiquity to give children names that referred to something a deity had done or to some epithet praising deity, we know that these attributes do not describe the person of the Messiah; nor do they confer deity on the Messiah. Rather, they are names of God, and they describe various ways in which God acts in the world. These names do not refer to the Messiah's make-up as being, except as they depict a being in unique relation to God and to other beings. They point to his special relation to God's work in the world. They form not an ontological but a "historical" statement, in the sense that the concerns are all with man and his actions and relations in this world.

In the Bible as a whole that is precisely the subject of Christology. This is true even in the Gospel of John, which so often has been the quarry for texts supporting incarnational theologies that in effect tend toward Christomonism. Yet we read: "God so loved the world that he gave his only Son, that whosoever believes . . . shall have eternal life" (John 3:16). That is, Jesus is to be understood as the specially adopted son of God, who has a vital part in God's work of giving life and delivering from death. Jesus has a special food from God, which is to enable people "to do the will of him who sent me, to accomplish his work" (John 4:32–34). Jesus said: "I am the light of the world; he that follows me will not walk in darkness, but will have the light of life." To the Pharisees, who charged that he was bearing false witness about himself, Jesus replied that his judgment is true, not because of himself, but because of him "who sent me" (John 8:12–16).

In classic Christian theology Christology has generally dealt with the divine and human natures of Christ and with his work of atonement and reconciliation. In the Bible, however, there is never a question of discussing Christ in and of himself; he is defined in the context of God's action in the world. Christology is always clearly relational.[1] The person of Christ is the turning point of time, God's time, filled with his purpose and work in his creation.

[1] Of course early Christological controversies were concerned pre-

1   Our Loss of God

Christology is a problem to many of our generation precisely because of its *theo*logical aspects. There is no lack of respect for Jesus Christ, but there is wonderment about the God who sent him. Our proclamation of God, our doctrine of God, in the Church has been weak precisely because of the confusion in our minds, so seldom confessed, about what real-life content we can put into the word "God." And confusion here means the death of faith.

In order to depict the desperate situation of our theologies at this point, allow me to refer to one characteristic of our time that appears to be central to all existential philosophies. This is pertinent because in the history of the western world, theologians have always been heavily involved in philosophy, and reflect in their own work current philosophical thinking.

Kierkegaard is acknowledged as the father of modern existentialists. He had this to say:[2]

> With the N.T. before me I ask myself the following question: how do we men, nowadays, stand in relation to the whole view of life expressed in the N.T.; has there not, by comparison with it, been a whole qualitative change in the race, and what it means to be a man?

> Yes there has, and nothing is easier to see.

> Where does the change lie? It is that the "in-and-for-itself," the absolute, has gone out of life, and reason has been put in its place . . .

cisely with the relationship of God to Christ, or vice versa. The philosophical background behind the language used was primarily ontological, however, rather than "existential," with the result that in subsequent theological discussion Christology had a dominant ontological aspect, a subject in and of itself, its primary relational aspects subdued.

[2] *The Journals of Kierkegaard* (tr. selected and with an Introduction by Alexander Dru [New York: Harper Torchbooks, 1959], pp. 218–219.

The "in-and-for-itself" and reason are related to one another inversely; where the one is the other is not.

Kierkegaard, an intellectual of intellectuals, does not mean that there is no thinking or reasoning in faith. Rather, he means that it is more normal for reason to talk *about* realities than to proclaim and confess them as truth in a context of actual human relationships.

The Danish philosopher had a great dislike of his contemporary Hegel. He called him "a miserable don . . . who had seen through the necessity of everything and got the whole thing off by heart." "Ye gods!" Kierkegaard exclaims.[3] He was radically against all the great philosophical systems of the past, which tried to explain everything. He said:[4]

> In relation to their systems most systematizers are like a man who builds an enormous castle and lives in a shack close by; they do not live in their own enormous systematic buildings. But spiritually that is a decisive objection. Spiritually speaking a man's thought must be the building in which he lives— otherwise everything is topsy-turvy.

Our very American thinker, William James, writing about "The Present Dilemma of Philosophy," used the same architectural figure to say the same thing:[5]

> The world of concrete personal experiences to which the street belongs [William James referred to this aspect of his thought as "street philosophy"] is multitudinous beyond imagination, tangled, muddy, painful and perplexed. The world to which your philosophy-professor introduced you is simple, clean and noble. The contradictions of real life are absent from it. Its architecture is classic. Principles of reason trace its outlines, logical necessities cement its parts. Purity and dignity are what it most expresses. It is a kind of marble temple shining on a hill.

[3] *Ibid.*, p. 238.
[4] *Ibid.*, p. 98.
[5] *Pragmatism* (New York: Meridian Books, 1955), pp. 27–28. I owe this reference and the point being made here to John Wild.

In point of fact . . . it is no explanation of our concrete universe, it is another thing altogether, a substitute for it, a remedy, a way of escape.

Its temperament, if I may use the word temperament here, is utterly alien to the temperament of existence in the concrete.

In other words—and this is basic to all modern existentialisms—traditional philosophy was too abstract, too artificial. Beginning with Plato the world of everyday living, the world of change, of war, of evil, of human beings living their daily lives—this was simply too ambiguous to be the real subject of philosophy. There was another world, more ordered behind or in this human chaos. But existentialists ask whether such thinking is proper for the philosopher. Philosophy ought to grow out of our present existence, if it is to mean anything. And this suggests that the great metaphysical systems of the past have to be discarded; they are much too abstract, unreal, unrelated to us, and unconvincing. The old ontological and other rational arguments for God's existence do not convince any longer.[6] Just to be able to think out something logically does not necessarily make it true. Since the days of Freud, we as human beings are known to be much too complex for reason to be singled out as an infallible instrument.

This is the context of thinking today. Various modern theologies affirm a similar viewpoint. The old systems are not for us. We must start where we are. Theology is an action of people who are reacting responsibly to their everyday world, the environment of relatedness with its past, present, and future in which they live.

Yet if we draw all basic categories from our existential life-world, how do we get to God? How is theology possible if metaphysics is impossible? Is not my life chaotic? How do I perceive God in it? In a world of war and social sickness, of bald-faced lies used as

[6] Pivotal here, of course, is the figure of Immanuel Kant. See, e.g., his treatment of the ontological argument in his *Critique of Pure Reason* (tr. by F. Max Miller; London: Macmillan, 1881), pp. 502 ff. See also Paul Tillich's discussion of the same subject in his *Systematic Theology*, Vol. I (Chicago: University of Chicago Press, 1951), pp. 204–210; and Donald R. Burrill, ed., *The Cosmological Arguments: A Spectrum of Opinion* (Doubleday Anchor Book, 1967).

diplomacy, of desperate poverty and the festering sores of the slum, where do I see God?

It is small wonder then that people talk about "the death of God," or that we have a generation of revolt, with many rejecting everything in the past, seeing only a vision of chaos, of human reality torn apart. To talk about the Biblical God in such a context is to use words that have no meaningful content for many. And there is a more widespread suspicion of the irrelevance of the Church and the synagogue in this situation than there is even of theology. We frequently hear apocalyptic statements to the effect that if the Church does not get with it, it will be dead by the end of the century.

To any Biblically oriented person there is truth in all these statements because the God of the Bible preserves a tension between his will and our world. The disillusion or disenchantment with our present common life, with our churches, and with the God talked about in the churches can be viewed as one aspect of the divine judgment upon us today. Since we suffer under "the curse of contemporaneity,"[7] in which anything to have value must be new, faith requires a renewed confrontation with our heritage to learn the identity and meaning of God.

II   Christomonism as One Theological Answer to Faith's Trouble

In modern times our problem with God has had major repercussions for theology. I focus here on only one of these. While *theo*logy, or meaningful talk about God, has weakened among Christians, varieties of Christology—even Jesusology—have grown stronger. Throughout Christian history the Kingdom of God and the sovereignty of God have most often been the subjects around which faith and its articulation have taken form. Yet today there is

---

[7] A phrase of Elton Trueblood's used in reference to current rejection of the past and all its works, and the deception and imprisonment of those who feel that they and their problems and actions are so new as to be completely unrelated to anything that previous generations knew or experienced.

a widespread feeling that this political terminology is improper or must be demythologized. One contemporary theologian in conversation put the issue as he saw it quite simply: "We cannot talk about God any more; but we can talk about Jesus."

By "Christomonism" I do *not* refer to any and every form of Christocentric piety and theology. Rather the reference is precisely to the sharp narrowing of religious attention implied in the remark just quoted from a contemporary theologian. Whether in devotional expression or in sophisticated theological statement, Christomonism sharply restricts revelation to Jesus Christ, so that anything to be said about God is either confined to, or secondary to, what is said about Christ.

There are surely several sources of Christomonism in the contemporary church. One obvious source is to be seen in the Christocentric theology of Karl Barth and, of a very different order, that of Rudolf Bultmann to which we shall return. Another is surely the very common Christian humanism of people inside the church and out, who have long since discarded theology as mumbo-jumbo, but see in Jesus a type of the good man for humanity, and in the Sermon on the Mount (Matt. 6–8) all the teaching one needs from the Bible about life. Edmund Wilson believed, for example, that the Dead Sea Scrolls were going to prove finally that the Jesus of dogma and revelation had to give way to the Jesus of history—not a god-man let down out of heaven or a being of miracle, but a human being in history and of history.[8] This was the substance of the contrived "controversy" over the Scrolls, at which Biblical scholars the world over looked on with amused amazement at its naîveté. Yet still another source of Christomonism is the Christian pietistic heritage.

Tendencies toward a Christ-mysticism or Christomonism have always been present in the Church. These tendencies, at least by emphasis, ascribe to Christ everything meaningful that one would affirm about God. Two familiar illustrations can be given:

The first is German Lutheran pietism, a devotionally centered and sharp reaction to excessive theological rationalism and un-

---

[8] See Edmund Wilson in *The New Yorker Magazine,* May 14, 1955; and subsequently *The Scrolls from the Dead Sea* (New York: Oxford University Press, 1955).

reality. This pietism furnished the words or texts immortalized by
J. S. Bach in his cantatas, B-Minor Mass, and St. Matthew Passion.
Bach's method was to have the Biblical text objectively presented
by a recitative. Then the solos and chorales explain what the story
meant and its impact on the believer. The music is so powerful and
so attuned to its text that, as all great art should do, it speaks
primarily to the whole person through his emotions, rather than
through the mind. Analyzed without the music, the text is often exceedingly sentimental, and is dominantly Christomonistic. Here are
illustrations from *The Passion of Our Lord According to St.
Matthew:*

After the reading of the story of the Last Supper, a soprano solo
affirms:

> I will give my heart to Thee;
> sink Thyself in it, my Salvation,
> I will submerge myself in Thee.
> And if the world is too small for Thee,
> Ah, then for me alone shalt Thou
> be more than world and Heaven.

This is addressed to Christ, who is here the whole divine reality in
earth and heaven. Following the story of Pilate's colloquy with the
people who demand Jesus' crucifixion, a chorale sings:

> How miraculous indeed is this punishment!
> The good shepherd suffers for his sheep;
> The Master, righteous as he is, pays the penalty
>   for his vassals!

After the crucifixion, the words of a bass aria are:

> Come, sweet Cross, I will say then:
> My Jesus, give it always to me.
> Should my pain become too heavy,
> Then help me to carry it myself.

Jesus here is the sole and sufficient object of piety and devotion.
Other dimensions of divine reality play no part. Jesus *is* divine
reality—and the theology can be called a devotional unitarianism.[9]

[9] The pietism of Calvinistic or Reformed circles, under the influence
of Calvin's central concern for "the knowledge of God," tended by

Contrast the text used in Handel's *Messiah* which could well serve as a summary of early apostolic preaching (the Jerusalem kerygma) as depicted in Acts. This is a very different thing, though Christocentric, from the Lutheran pietistic texts used by Bach. The first part provides the Old Testament setting of the Christ-event. Then the passion of Christ is given indirectly in the second part, many of the verses used being taken from the Old Testament, especially from Isaiah 53. The climax is reached in the "Hallelujah Chorus," the text of which provides the mood of the whole:

> Hallelujah. The Kingdom of this world is become
> the Kingdom of our Lord and of His Christ;
> And He shall reign forever and ever.

A second illustration can be found in the evangelistic songs, the "old" Gospel hymns, of the nineteenth century, those written particularly between about 1830 and 1880, though their type is still composed to this day.

There is Fanny J. Crosby (1823–1915), a blind lady, writing "Blessed assurance, Jesus is mine!" "Asleep in the arms of Jesus," and:

> I am thine, O Lord, I have heard thy voice,
> And it told thy love to me;
> But I long to rise in the arms of faith
> And be closer drawn to thee.
>
> Draw me nearer, nearer, blessed Lord,
> To the cross where thou hast died. . . .

Or there are: "What a Friend we have in Jesus" (Joseph Scriven, 1857), "I love to tell the story . . . of Jesus and His Glory"

---

contrast to be centered in God and the Holy Spirit, sometimes almost at the expense of Christology because of a great concern over those who sought to love Jesus without serving God. See the illuminating work of James R. Tanis, *Dutch Calvinistic Pietism in the Middle Colonies: A Study in the Life and Theology of Theodorus Jacobus Freylinghuysen* ('S-Gravenhage, Holland: Martinus Nijhoff, 1967), esp. the Introduction; and pp. 97 ff. See also H. R. Niebuhr on the Three Unitarianisms in Christianity in "The Doctrine of the Trinity and the Unity of the Church," *Theology Today*, Vol. III.3 (Oct., 1946), pp. 371–384.

(Katherine Hankey, 1874), "I need thee every hour, most gracious Lord" (Annie S. Hawks, 1872), "Yield not to temptation. . . . Look ever to Jesus—He will carry you through" (Horatio R. Palmer, 1868), "I've found a Friend, oh, such a Friend!" (James G. Small, 1866), "Just as I am, without one plea But that thy blood was shed for me" (Charlotte Elliott, 1836), "Take the name of Jesus with you" (Lydia Baxter, 1809–1874), "My faith looks up to Thee, Thou Lamb of Calvary" (Ray Palmer, 1830), "Hark! the voice of Jesus calling" (Daniel March, 1868), "Softly and tenderly Jesus is calling" (Will L. Thompson, n.d.), "We would see Jesus" (Anna B. Warner, 1852), "Stand up, stand up for Jesus" (George Duffield, 1858), etc.

A hymn by C. Austin Miles (1868–1946), "In the Garden," has this refrain:

> And He walks with me, and He talks with me,
> And He tells me I am His own,
> And the joy we share as we tarry there
> None other has ever known.

Such hymns are warm, very personal, very devotional, and they are an important part of the evangelistic heritage of our American churches in the days of their most rapid expansion. It is not that their authors are antitrinitarian, or that they did not believe in God. But a focusing of religious attention on God was simply unnecessary. Jesus fulfilled all the requirements of the Christian's devotion, as he filled almost completely the Christian's perspective of divinity in action.

III   *A Unitarianism of the Second Person*

We have noted two examples of Christomonism in the Christian pietism of the past. We shall now briefly examine examples from contemporary theology (parts III and IV in this chapter), all of which in one way of another show the influence of Barth.

As background it may be remarked that since Immanuel Kant shifted the main issues of theology from the "theoretical reason" to the "practical reason," it is not surprising that many modern intellectuals should become suspicious of the objective reality behind the deductions of the "practical reason."

Ludwig Feuerbach (1804–1872) in *The Essence of Christianity* has given eloquent expression to these suspicions. God, he claims, is nothing but a projected image of man. "The object of any subject is nothing else than the subject's own nature taken objectively."[10] Theologically, his projection theory is expounded as follows:

> Man—this is the mystery of religion—projects his being into objectivity, and then again makes himself an object to this projected image of himself thus converted into a subject; he thinks of himself as an object to himself, but as the object of an object, of another being than himself. Thus here, Man is an object of God.[11]

Christian theologians would naturally be expected to counter such a position by speaking about revelation. In Barthian "neo-orthodoxy," however, there is a great sensitivity to the ambiguity in the term "revelation" when used of the world generally, whether of nature or of human religions. Barthians appear to feel that this difficulty is overcome when revelation is centered in Jesus Christ, and a discontinuity is claimed between the revelation in Christ and the worlds of nature and of the religions.[12]

It is unnecessary here to expound on the Barthian influence over the world church. It was so noticeably pervasive, for example, among the Europeans at the First Assembly of the World Council of Churches, meeting in 1948 at Amsterdam, that I as an observer returned to this country to speak of the "new theology" then as a "new monotheism based on Christ." With his special facility in ex-

[10] Tr. by George Eliot (New York: Harper & Row, 1957), p. 12.

[11] *Ibid.*, pp. 29–30.

[12] See, e.g., Emil Brunner's debate with Barth in *Natur und Gnade zum Gespräch mit Karl Barth* (Zurich: Zwingli Verlag, n.d.). The English ed. is *Natural Theology* (London: Geoffrey Bles, 1946). Cf. Barth's "The Revelation of God and the Abolition of Religion" in *Church Dogmatics*, Vol. I, Part 2 (New York: Charles Scribner's Sons, 1956), pp. 280 ff.

pression Elton Trueblood described the position at Amsterdam more aptly as a "new unitarianism of the Second Person."[13]

An unexpected example of the style of theology in question appears in the *Confession of 1967* adopted by the United Presbyterian Church in the United States of America. It is unexpected because one would never think of discovering such a definite tendency toward Christomonism in a denomination that so prides itself on being an American spiritual heir of John Calvin.[14] Nevertheless, it represents a responsible doctrinal statement from a church that stands squarely in the center of the great Protestant consensus today.[15]

Criticism of this fine document is difficult and perhaps unfair. The final edition as adopted is well-written. It has been so repeatedly revised and improved that the original theological tendencies of the drafting committee have been to a large extent blurred, and properly so. Yet certain of these tendencies remain.

One of these is the careful avoidance of language drawn from

[13] Without giving voluminous bibliography here, may I simply direct attention to a small book by the former General Secretary of the WCC: W. A. Visser 't Hooft, *The Kingship of Christ* (New York, Harper & Brothers, 1948). The confessional standard for member churches adopted at the Amsterdam Assembly was belief in Jesus Christ as "God and Savior." This was considerably modified in 1961 at the New Delhi Assembly, as follows: "The World Council of Churches is a fellowship of churches which confess the Lord Jesus Christ as God and Savior *according to the Scriptures* [italics mine] and therefore seek to fulfill together their common calling to the glory of the one God, Father, Son and Holy Spirit" (*New Delhi Report;* New York: Association Press, 1962, p. 152).

[14] I draw here on a certain personal knowledge because as a member of the Committee appointed to write the first draft of the Confession, I was in regular attendance at the meetings during its first three years of work.

[15] The document in question is found in the *Minutes of the General Assembly of the United Presbyterian Church in the United States of America,* Part I. *Journal* (Philadelphia: Office of the General Assembly of the United Presbyterian Church in the United States of America, 1965), pp. 303 ff., esp. pp. 326–341; and as finally adopted, *ibid.,* 1967, pp. 731–740.

the political realm. Not even the word "Lord" is used in relation to either Christ or God, except in a quoted phrase of Scripture. There are a few uses of the terms "victory," "judgment," and "obedience." The term "kingdom" appears only in the final two paragraphs before the devotional ascription of praise. Since the "sovereignty" of God and the "kingdom" of God have been pivotal in Calvin and in his theological descendants, there must have been a strong tendency at work in these sons of Calvin on the committee to cause them to use a different pattern of organization, so that terms of political origin are incidental, and "kingdom" appears only at the end, almost like a gloss, or like something rewritten after the completion of the document, or like what the late Paul Haupt of Johns Hopkins University was accustomed to refer to as "a euphemistic liturgical appendage." A frequent sign of Christomonism is the rejection of political language as an appropriate model for the God made known in Christ.

Second, the pattern of organization is clear from the very beginning. In keeping with one trend in modern theology this pattern is Christological. An attempt is made to set it in a trinitarian context by the use of the words, "The grace of our Lord Jesus Christ and the love of God and the communion of the Holy Spirit" (2 Cor. 13:14), these phrases providing the subheads of the first part. Yet in general, statements about God are secondary in the Confession to statements about Christ and his reconciling work. Three illustrations of this overriding Christology within the committee can be cited:

The first, it seems to me, was a rather clever avoidance of the fundamentalist issue. This was aptly and clearly expounded by the committee's chairman, Edward A. Dowey, during the debate on the Confession in the General Assembly, meeting in Boston during May, 1966. The Bible as a whole is only in a secondary or derived sense "The Word of God." Instead, in the words of the Confession,

> The one sufficient revelation of God is Jesus Christ, the Word of God incarnate, to whom the Holy Spirit bears unique and authoritative witness through the Holy Scriptures. . . .

This is a very exclusive and highly Barthian statement, which seems to me to characterize the tendency of the document as a whole.

A second illustration is the manner in which the Confession begins almost every subject it raises by relating it immediately to Christ, who forms the setting of the discussion. References to God abound, but it is clear that to the original framers of the Confession such references receive content *only* from what one can say about Christ. The complexity of the divine working in the world, suggested by both the Bible and the Church's attempt to summarize the Bible in a trinitarian, rather than a unitarian, pattern, is neglected. The result in early editions of the document was almost completely inner-group talk, while references to other people and religions on the earth were omitted. For this reason I was able to use the document in theology seminars as a perfect example of what H. Richard Niebuhr has called "Christian henotheism."[16] Only after criticism was this characteristic to some extent eliminated in the final rewritings.

A third illustration is the new life which Christians have in Christ. "The reconciling work of Jesus," we are told, "was the supreme crisis in the life of mankind. His cross and resurrection become personal crisis and present hope for men when the gospel is proclaimed and believed." The new life takes shape in a community; it does not release one from conflict; it finds its direction in the life of Jesus, his deeds and words; the members of the church are emissaries of peace and seek the good of man; and life in Christ is life eternal.

This interpretation, again very Barthian, is very shallow as re-

[16] *Radical Monotheism and Western Culture* (New York: Harper & Row, 1960), esp. pp. 58–60. Niebuhr claims that "henotheism in Christianity tends to take one of two forms, the Church-centered or Christ-centered form." In his view the second results when the Lordship of Christ is substituted for the Lordship of God. Christ is invested "with such absolute significance that his relation to the One beyond himself is so slurred over that he becomes the center of value and the object of loyalty. The confidence that is expected of Christians is confidence in him. The formulation of the confidence in creed and theology becomes a set of assertions about Jesus Christ. Theology is turned into Christology."

gards time. At one point only has all that is significant for man occurred. There is no background or foreground. There is no sense of the history of civilization, or of the future history of man, as divinely directed for the sake of man's humanity. Moses and the prophets lived in vain, for God through them taught us little that is worth mentioning in this connection. Man in all his relations with all his institutions is supposed to find his life at one point in time which is full of the present and of eternal life, but has no significant past and no future history. As for other religions, they only make us see the human character of Christianity as a religion. The gift of God in Christ is for all men and all religions and for men with no religion; it is the fullness of revelation.

A major question to be asked of the Confession of 1967 is whether it can serve as an instrument for the quickening of faith in our everyday world, within the situation in which we now live. To be sure, it is in clear, readable English. Yet do the words mean anything concrete to us? I would say, not a great deal; we still must do the hard part, which is to translate its words into the situation of historical existence that we face daily. The Confession is still too much under the influence of the older theology, where the style was impersonal, generalized, abstract, where it was thought possible to express truths as universals valid for every time and place. Yet out of tune as this generalized theology of universals is in our day, the problem is made so much worse by a Christology that funnels virtually every topic about man or God through itself, leaving us with a theology without depth or background in history or in the vast variety of human experience in civilization, nor in hope within that civilization, apart from a nonhistorical life eternal.

Let me digress momentarily on the problem of confession in our time. Two lessons from the Bible would be helpful if we would take them seriously.

The first is that confession always arises out of concrete personal experience, which is either taken before God or else used as the ground for praise, confession, or a meditation or inquiry before God. And it takes place before the congregation, or even before the world of all men. This is particularly clear in the Psalms, where even generalized liturgical expressions have concrete images behind them that speak directly to immediate experience. In the words of Amos N. Wilder: "The Old Testament is dramatic in the sense that it records graphically the encounter and dialogue of God with men in relation to concrete historical scenes and actions. The New Testament literature and the Christian religion itself partake of this dramatic substance. . . . It is not surprising that the rhetoric of the first believers reflects this dynamic situation."[17] The prominence of free narration or of recital in the hymns of praise and in covenant renewal ceremonies of Israel is today well known and often commented on.[18]

Indeed, it is questionable whether the divine reality to which the Bible bears witness can actually be communicated in any other manner. Confession, then, is not very meaningful unless it has an immediacy to actual, experienced situations, the context being what William James called "street philosophy." And the language must partake of a dialogue form with a speaker, speaking something to be heard.[19]

A second Scriptural lesson is the point with which I began. It is that the Christological language of the Bible is always relational. It refers to the Messiah's role in the context of the larger work of God, and is accompanied generally by a reference of immediate import to the hearer in his particular situation. For example, the messianic passages of Isaiah 9 and 11 appear to have been addressed to people in Jerusalem in 734 B.C., when during the threat of invasion the hearts of king and people "shook as the trees of the forest shake before the wind" (Isa. 7:2). The Apostle Paul

[17] *The Language of the Gospel* (New York: Harper & Row, 1964), p. 59. Note also W. Zimmerli, "Die Weisung des Alten Testamentes zum Geschäft der Sprache," *Das Problem der Sprache in Theologie und Kirche* (ed. W. Schneemelcher; Berlin: A. Töpelmann, 1959), pp. 1–20.

[18] The technical name for confession as the recital of God's mighty acts toward Israel in services of worship may well have been *tôdāh,* while *hôdāh* in such contexts refers to the praise of God by recital of events. This has been convincingly argued by David W. Kerr in his unpublished Harvard doctoral dissertation, *The Meaning of the Words* Hôdāh *and* Tôdāh *in the Old Testament* (1966).

[19] Cf. Emil Brunner, *The Divine-Human Encounter* (Philadelphia: Westminster Press, 1943), pp. 45 ff.

in reciting the *Kenosis* hymn in Philippians 2:5–11 both preceded and followed it by admonitions concerning how Christians must act toward one another and how they must look upon their own lives, "for God is at work in you both to will and to work for his good pleasure" (Phil. 2:13).

At a time when faith in God is a central problem for the faithful, it is not necessarily helpful to say a great deal about Christ if little can be said about God. In any traditional sense *Christo*-centricity is meaningless without a prior *theo*centricity. It can be a purely humanistic, nontheistic perspective with a positivist criterion of meaning. What is stressed here, however, is the use of Christocentricity in current theologies as an attempted answer to the modern skepticism about divine transcendence. The next step from such a theology is the Christian "death of God" theologians. All have a high respect for Christ, but can say nothing positive about God, and their attempts at theology at that point are certainly not impressive. I do not see how such attempts are any ground for faith, unless faith is only optimism.

IV Existentialist Christomonism and the Old Testament

From the examples of types of Christocentricity called Christomonism thus far given, the stress has been on their simplistic, unrealistic and nonhistorical nature. Consequently, they really have little to say to anyone who is unable to make any positive affirmation about God in our time. As a result, they are simply unable to come to any real understanding of our existence as historical people.

In this section stress is to be laid upon the abstract picture of Jesus which is thus created because he is not really a historical person with a background in which his life is given meaning. If Jesus' life has no setting in the Old Testament, for example, if God said nothing through Israel to which Jesus related himself as fulfillment, then what and who is Jesus? As an extreme example of a highly artificial, abstract Christ, with no meaningful Old Testament background, no history, only a punctiform "eschatological deed of forgiveness"—where even the word "eschatological"

does not mean what the English term would lead one to suppose—
let us turn to the existentialist Christomonism of Rudolf Bultmann.

Professor Bernhard W. Anderson, now at Princeton Theological
Seminary, during a visit to Germany, happened upon an essay by
Rudolf Bultmann on "The Significance of the Old Testament for
the Christian Faith."[20] It had escaped serious attention, perhaps
because of the subsequent debate on Bultmann's program for
demythologizing of the New Testament. Anderson was so surprised
by the essay that with Bultmann's permission he arranged a "panel
discussion" on the author's views with regard to the Old Testament. The result was a significant volume, published in 1963 under
the title *The Old Testament and Christian Faith*.[21] In this volume
many of the most pressing issues of today's theological spectrum
are raised for discussion. It is worthwhile to review briefly Bultmann's provocative position in order to ascertain both the nature
and the effects of a particularly influential type of Christomonism.

The first thing an Old Testament scholar notices in Bultmann's
essay is the *presupposition* that the Old and New Testaments, while
obviously related, are two different religions standing only in historical continuity.

> In so far as the phenomenon of primitive Christianity cannot
> be understood as a stage in the unfolding development of Old
> Testament religion, extraneous influences from the Orient and
> from Greek tradition are invoked. The complex phenomenon
> of primitive Christianity then appears as the result of the
> whole ancient history of religion in which the Old Testament
> is only one, albeit an essential factor.[22]

From one point of view any historical phenomenon is complex
and is in continual action and interaction with its environment.
Yet it is simply not historically accurate to assert flatly that primi-

[20] Published in 1933 in the first volume of Bultmann's *Glauben und
Verstehen*.

[21] Bernhard W. Anderson, ed. (New York: Harper & Row, 1963).
The volume's first chapter is a translation of Bultmann's original essay;
there follows discussion of the subject by twelve other scholars on both
the European and the American sides of the Atlantic.

[22] *Ibid.*, p. 8, n. 1.

tive Christianity was a "different religion" from that of Israel. The Old Testament is the cradle of the Christian movement, in which the basic issues are formulated to which the Christian movement addressed itself. The early Christians thought of themselves as being in organic continuity of faith and divine action with the Old Testament. To be sure, Jesus himself appears in the tradition as uncomfortable with the title of Messiah of Israel, but the early Church had no difficulty with the conception after the resurrection. In his life Jesus was the Suffering Servant, and the royal or messianic language was clearly assumed to apply to his post-resurrection "ascension to the right hand of God"—political or messianic language from Israel's royal theology, taken from Psalm 110. In any event,

> the evidence is also convincing that Jesus and the primitive Church believed that Israel would have no other Messiah, no other fulfillment. . . . The conviction of the New Testament is that the history of Israel, which is the history of its encounter with God, should have brought Israel to the point of recognition. By implication, it is suggested that this same history should bring anyone to the point of recognition. It is the history of Israel that isolates Jesus Christ from any figures in the ancient and modern world who might wear enough of his features to confuse those who seek vaguely what he brings. . . . It is remarkable, it is even sharply surprising, when one reflects that only as the Savior of Israel can Jesus be recognized as none of these other things.[23]

If one searches through Bultmann's writings to discover what it is that leads him to the presupposition of two religions, there would appear to be many factors involved. Yet surely the chief one is his definition of the central characteristic of the New Testament in distinction to the Old Testament. What is the specifically Christian content of the New Testament? Bultmann states that it is "the idea that *man's relation to God is bound to the person of Jesus.*" His question then follows: "Can the idea be eliminated that God is accessible only in Jesus Christ? Or does the Christian faith stand or fall with this assertion?" He claims that there can be no doubt

[23] John L. McKenzie, S.J., *ibid.*, pp. 108–109.

whatever that this is the specifically Christian element, which requires a "critical reduction" so that things not in accord with it
are eliminated. Without it "the religion that remains is a refined
Judaism or a humanism." Hence the question with regard to the
Old Testament must be "whether the Old Testament still has a
meaning for the faith which perceives in Jesus Christ the revelation
of God."[24]

From such a Christomonistic standpoint the answer to the question of the significance of the Old Testament for the Christian
faith is obvious from the start: "Jesus is God's demonstration of
grace in a manner which is fundamentally different from the demonstration of divine grace attested in the Old Testament."[25] The
"Word of God" in the Old Testament appears only when the
"understanding of existence . . . is the same as that of the New
Testament." It would seem that for Bultmann the basic problem
is that the grace of God in the Old Testament is grasped in an
ethnic history (*Volksgeschichte*), whereas Christ is God's "eschatological deed of forgiveness," which puts an end to all ethnic history.
We even read this astounding statement: "Israel's history is not
our history, and in so far as God has shown his grace in that history, such grace is not meant for us. . . . This means, however,
that *to us the history of Israel is not history of revelation*. The
events which meant something for Israel, which were God's Word,
mean nothing more to us." Historically, they may contribute to
us as "episodes which form a part of our Occidental history. In
the same sense, however, it can be said that the Spartans fell at
Thermopylae for us and that Socrates drank the hemlock for us."
The Old Testament, "freed from its history," can be proclaimed
in the Church as God's Word only when the Church finds in it
"what is already known from the revelation in Jesus Christ."[26]

The stress on the ethnic nature of the Old Testament in this re-

[24] *Ibid., pp.* 11–13.
[25] *Ibid.,* p. 29. These words and those quoted in the next sentence
were italicized by Bultmann in the original, but the italics are omitted
here as unnecessary.
[26] *Ibid.,* pp. 30–35. Italics are Bultmann's.

gard is peculiar and may have been influenced unconsciously by
the situation in central Europe at the time when the essay was
written. The Church has always claimed that Israel could never
be understood solely on ethnic grounds but was a special people
created by God for the world's sake. Israel's election was for the
purpose of providing a source of blessing to the nations (Gen.
12:3; Jer. 4:2):

> I have given you as a covenant to the people,
>   a light to the nations,
>   to open the eyes that are blind.
>   (Isa. 42:6–7)[27]

Consequently, Israel's reason for being was more akin to that of
the Church or "people of God" than to that of nation among nations. As a result, the Church without difficulty saw itself as the
real successor to the assembly of God, the new "people of God"
formed by God's act in Christ, and the true heirs of Abraham by
faith.

That the mighty acts of God in the Old Testament, the *magnalia
Dei* of the history and confessions, are not special events wrought
for us as Christians is a most peculiar claim, one that has the
whole weight of Christian history and liturgy *against* it. The great
Easter hymn of John of Damascus (8th cent.), still in frequent
use at least in Anglican and American Episcopalian services, is
one such example. Its first stanza is as follows:

> Come, ye faithful, raise the strain
> Of triumphant gladness!
> God hath brought his Israel
> Into joy from sadness;
> Loosed from Pharaoh's bitter yoke,
> Jacob's sons and daughters,
> Led them with unmoistened foot
> Through the Red Sea Waters.

---

[27] This passage was certainly lifted into the Christian context very
early (cf. Luke 2:29–32), and as the *Nunc Dimittis* has continued in
Christian worship until this day.

A familiar and much-loved Advent hymn, based on ancient Latin antiphons, is *Veni Emmanuel.* Its first stanza reads:

> O come, O come, Emmanuel,
> And ransom captive Israel;
> That mourns in lonely exile here,
> Until the Son of God appear.

If Israel's events are not Christian events, how are we to interpret such hymns? How are we to understand the Puritan use of these events to interpret their history in New England? The crossing of the sea and the journey through the wilderness to the Promised Land have played a vital and formative role in the interpretation of the American experience.[28] The crossing of the sea and the crossing of the Jordan have always been used in Christian hymnody. Here is an example from a favorite hymn in the American churches:

> When through the deep waters I call thee to go,
> The rivers of woe shall not thee overflow;
> For I will be with thee thy troubles to bless
> And sanctify to thee thy deepest distress.[29]

And, of course, the American Negro spirituals are saturated with allusions to Old Testament people, places, and events. Indeed, the use of the Old Testament in the history of Christian art in itself belies the Bultmann statement. The liberation from slavery and the journey through the wilderness to the promised land have often been individualized for a person's life, death, and resurrection, but they can never be simplistically reduced to what is already known from the revelation in Jesus Christ as Bultmann defines that revelation.

Is this type of usage rejected by Bultmann as significant because

---

[28] Rather than multiply references on something so familiar, I shall simply refer to the book by my colleague George H. Williams, *Wilderness and Paradise in Christian Thought* (New York: Harper & Row, 1962).

[29] From "How firm a foundation," published in a selection of hymns in 1787 called "Rippon's Selection."

it violates his rule that the Old Testament be used in its original sense, though without its original reference to the Israelite people and their history, and thus that every form of allegory be discontinued? Such a program would not only cut Christians off completely from any shared experience with the Jews; the question must be asked whether the whole history of the Christian use of the Old Testament is not suspect in Bultmann's position. Would not the point be better stated that the great events of revelation are what they are because they have windows and mirrors within them whereby human experiences in different times and places can be illumined? Like Leviathan have they not for many become archetypes lifted to universal, even cosmic, dimensions? And did not this manner of reference begin within Israel's own history itself?

Furthermore, Bultmann's Christomonism furnishes the framework for his question about the Old Testament: Since Christ is the revelation of God, has the Old Testament any existential meaning for the Christian? One would have thought that the primary question would concern itself with the identity of God and of his purpose, or of the teleology he has placed in history. For it is in the context of this historical teleology that the life of Christ has meaning. The Christ of Bultmann as "the eschatological deed of forgiveness" is no longer an actual flesh-and-blood individual, but an abstraction, a concept of value, not for history, but solely for the individual's "existential situation"—if this situation is not in itself a mythology.

In other words, Christomonism here plays a real role in the dehistoricizing of the Bible, and in the sharp separation that Bultmann insists on making between meaningful history (*geschichte*) and material or merely "factual history" (*historie*). The fact that this artificial separation is made by Bultmann, that his viewpoint ends with no history, no society, and few symbolic language patterns permissible in communication, has often been commented on. The occasion for such radical reductionism is usually cited as the existentialist philosophical base of the theology. The point here is to insist that Christomonism is an important factor in the deficiencies of the viewpoint as theology. Certainly it is a vital ingredient in the theology's inability to make significant use of the Old Testament.

Yet a strongly sympathetic chord is struck in me when Bultmann insists that the study of history is not simply the arrangement of phenomena in their place. He writes: "A genuinely historical inquiry of Plato, for instance, is not one that seeks to understand Plato in the context of a history of problems, but rather one that intends to learn in dialogue with him what man is and how he is to exist." Thus the Old Testament is to be "interpreted in terms of the question of *what basic possibility it presents for an understanding of human existence (Daseinsverständnis)*."[30] Does not this insistence bring us into the environment of William James' "street philosophy," that is, out of the marble palace that reason constructs into the context of everyday life as we live it?

As is well-known, Bultmann insists that "the concept 'existence' must be the methodological starting point of theology."[31] Yet the particular categories of existentialism he draws from Heidegger are concerned with the ultimates of life and death, with the anxiety of existence in the face of nonexistence, and with the problem of "authentic" self-understanding, of "authentic existence." The question arises whether these concerns are any nearer one's actual living context than was reason's marble palace. To be sure, each human being is concerned with his "existence" and at various times he is forced to confront death. Yet what has surprised me in the examination of this type of existentialism is that it does not describe the life I daily live. I exist in a context of activity and relationships where for the most part death is not a real factor affecting my decisions, nor is the fear of nonbeing a substantially restricting or influential force. Instead, I have the power to push that type of anxiety far into the background and so seal it off that it does not disturb my current existence with its relationships and duties. To suggest that this point may beg the question because, insofar as I am able to push such ultimate concerns from my consciousness, I

---

[30] Bultmann, *loc. cit.*, pp. 13–14. The italics are Bultmann's.
[31] So, e.g., in "The Historicity of Man and Faith," *Existence and Faith* (S. M. Ogden, ed. and tr.; New York: Meridian Books, 1960), p. 92.

am living an inauthentic existence requires an artificial definition of authentic existence. I did not choose to be born. I cannot control my destiny in death. Instead, these mysteries are hidden in the God who calls me to responsible vocation now in the sure hope of a future. Is not some such formulation, which is certainly central to the Biblical view of life, the actual setting of my existence and therefore authentic?

In other words, the question here concerns the actual reality of the term "existence" as it has been used in existential theology. Is it actually any less an artificial construct of the mind than the classical systems it has sought to replace? Are there not different varieties of existentialism that make a more serious attempt to depict the life I as an individual actually live in its authentic dimensions? When in Genesis 2—3, and in the Bible as a whole, the basic issues of life and death are seen with their ambiguities, with their duties and blessings, with promise, defeat, judgment, and hope—is this not a rather realistic insight into our living world as it really is? Is it, therefore, inauthentic?

In any event, existential Christomonism is no more helpful than any other Christomonism for the problems of faith and its articulation today. Let it be said, however, that it would be inappropriate at this point to attempt a precise definition of the various kinds of Christomonism that must be considered bad theology, or to draw a precise line between acceptable and unacceptable varieties of Christocentrism. This is too relative a matter, and Christianity permits great variety within its many forms. Examples have been pointed to above of thinking and devotional expression that cannot deal with the Old Testament and therefore with the whole problem of faith and history and with the sociopolitical context of our life together. This should be enough for an Old Testament scholar to say.

Let this chapter end with rather sweeping conclusions, which for some are overstatements of the situation: If the root problem of faith is whether any meaningul content for the term "God" exists at all, then it would appear that types of Christomonism merely complicate rather than resolve faith's problems. Furthermore, it can surely be said that almost any type of Christomonism finds itself in difficulty with the Christian doctrine of the Trinity. If that doctrine is to be taken seriously, it certainly implies a complexity in God's dealing with the world, which no monism can really handle. If the Trinity is primarily an attempt to summarize the Biblical understanding of deity in action, then clearly the Old Testament is a vital part of what is being summarized. And Christomonism is much too problematic in its capacity to deal adequately with Israel or with historical revelation. Surely the Church is not defenseless at these points. Has it not vast resources in its heritage that are largely untapped? In what follows a few suggestions drawn chiefly from the Old Testament will be presented.[32]

[32] That is, an Old Testament scholar has a great deal to say of importance to theology, unless the theological importance of Israel is excluded at the start.

2

Revelation and Theology

NOT ONLY must an Old Testament scholar protest against Christomonism as a substitute for a theology of the divine initiative in history, the only theology that can handle the Old and New Testaments together. He must also raise the question of the nature of revelation in such a way that the task of theology itself is challenged. In order to focus on the central issues it may be helpful to refer to certain recent discussions in the field of Old Testament theology.

I

Major modern contributions to this discipline belong to a comparatively brief period between the publication of the first volume of Walter Eichrodt's *Theologie des Alten Testaments* in 1933[1] and the second volume of Gerhard von Rad's *Theologie des Alten Testaments* in 1960.[2] These works are the greatest achievements of this century in their field. They differ radically, and von Rad's work, written twenty years later than Eichrodt's, has the advantage of working within the particular scholarly tradition that has had the most influence on theology in our time. This school of scholarship in both the Old and New Testaments has emphasized what has

[1] Tr. into English as *Theology of the Old Testament* by J. A. Baker from the 6th German ed. (1959), with author's revisions to Nov., 1960 (Philadelphia: Westminster Press, 1961). Vol. II (1939), tr. into English by J. A. Baker from the 5th German ed. (1964) (Philadelphia: Westminster Press, 1967).

[2] Vol. I (1957), tr. by D. M. G. Stalker (New York: Harper & Row, 1962); Vol. II (1965).

been called *heilsgeschichte* or kerygma as the central and characterizing element of the Bible. The emphasis has insisted that revelation is by event, that it is never propositional, that it cannot be systematized, indeed that systems represent a type of thinking that may be actually antithetical to the Reality to which the Bible bears witness.

Some years ago I had occasion to ask the late Emil Brunner what he considered his most original and creative theological work. His answer was surprising. He said it was his small *The Divine-Human Encounter,*[3] that it was a fresh discovery to him and a joy to write. In his Foreword Brunner writes of making a discovery of vast importance to both theology and the life of the Church. He says:

> The Biblical conception of truth is: truth is encounter. Applying this knowledge in all spheres of Church doctrine and practice is of direct and unforeseen import; in this application I am aware that I have made only a modest beginning. But surely I may hope that this first advance will be of interest to all who take seriously the Reformation interpretation of Scripture. If my thesis in these lectures really represents faithfully the Biblical understanding of truth, then indeed much of our thinking and action in the Church must be different from what we have been accustomed to for centuries.[4]

The theme of his lectures began as an analysis of the objective and the subjective in Christian faith. This led to reflection on the Biblical concept of truth and to a statement that "our message of salvation and also of the Church's task is still burdened with the Subject-Object antithesis which originated in Greek philosophy."[5] God in the Bible is not a subject to be analyzed doctrinally in and for himself (*Gott-an-sich*); neither is man (*Menschen-an-sich*). "The God who approaches man is precisely the meaning of the doctrine of

[3] The chapters of this book were first presented as lectures at the University of Uppsala in the fall of 1937 under the arresting title, *Wahrheit als Begegnung:* tr. by A. W. Loos and published under the English title by Westminster Press, Philadelphia, in 1943.

[4] *Ibid.,* p. 7.

[5] *Loc. cit.*

the Triune God; . . . man, even in his natural being, is always the man who comes from God [and this] is the meaning of the doctrine of the image of God and of original sin."

This fact leads directly to another:

> That in the Bible this two-sided relation between God and man is not developed as doctrine, but rather is set forth as happening in a story. The relation between God and man and between man and God is not of such a kind that doctrine can adequately express it in abstract formulas. . . . It is not a timeless or static relation, arising from the world of ideas. . . : rather the relation is an event, and hence narration is the proper form to describe it. The decisive word-form in the language of the Bible is not the substantive, as in Greek, but the verb, the word of action. The thought of the Bible is not substantival, neuter and abstract, but verbal, historical and personal. Its concern is not with a relation which exists in and for itself, but with a relation which (so they say) occurs. God "steps" into the world, in relation to men: . . . He acts always in relation *to them,* and He always *acts.*[6]

Furthermore, Brunner continues:

> The revelation of God to men is the decisive element in what God does for them. And on the other hand the knowledge of God is the decisive element in the relation to be realized between man and God. . . . The event which is the relation between God and man hence is always an act of revelation: likewise the event which is the relation between man and God is always a relation based on knowing. For this reason the content of Scriptures, as narration about this relation . . . is always a history of revealing and knowing.[7]

Thus the narration of the Bible is not an added or incidental feature of the literature. It is the indispensable way of presenting Biblical "truth" because "knowledge and act, knowing and *happening* are . . . a single process."[8]

[6] *Ibid.,* pp. 45–48.
[7] *Ibid.,* pp. 51–52.
[8] *Ibid.,* p. 64.

Here was the first sophisticated modern theologian I had encountered who did not dismiss the event-narrative form in the Bible as something unimportant, as a primitive mythopoetry from which truth-for-us is to be abstracted as the kernel from the nut. Instead, the nature of the Bible's revelation, of the Bible's "truth," can be communicated only by the recital of events that contain, transmit, bear witness to God's acts of relating himself to people in time, in history, when seen by the illumined eye. No wonder Brunner felt this to be an important insight. And it was one ingredient in my own attempt to see Biblical theology as *sui generis,* different in kind from what western people have known as theology. It was, I claimed, a "theology of recital."[9]

Another ingredient in my attempt during the years 1948–1952 to reconceive the nature of Old Testament theology was Gerhard von Rad's highly original and now basic monograph, *The Problem of the Hexateuch.*[10] This was first published in Germany in 1938, and not more than one or two copies reached this country before the war. After the war, it was virtually unavailable. Fortunately, the thesis of the monograph was summarized in the Introduction to von Rad's commentary on Genesis so that I was able to give an account of it in a review article published in 1950.[11] One of von Rad's basic concerns is what unifies the Hexateuch, considering the vast variety in types of material within it. This variety, he says,

[9] G. Ernest Wright, *God Who Acts: Biblical Theology as Recital* (London: SCM Press, 1952; 7th impression, 1964).

[10] The monograph was originally published as Vol. XXVI of the *Beiträge zur Wissenschaft vom Alten und Neuen Testament,* 4th series (Stuttgart, 1938). It was reprinted in von Rad's *Gesammelte Studien zum Alten Testaments* (Munich: Kaiser Verlag, 1958) and is now tr. into English by E. W. T. Dicken, in *The Problem of the Hexateuch and Other Essays* (New York: McGraw-Hill, 1966).

[11] "Recent European Study in the Pentateuch," *Journal of Bible and Religion,* Vol. 18.4 (Oct., 1950), pp. 216–224. The first fascicule of von Rad's *Das Erste Buch Mose,* containing the Introduction, was published in the commentary series *Das Alte Testament Deutsch* (ed. by V. Herntrich and A. Weiser) in Göttingen during 1949. The whole commentary is now available in an English tr. by J. H. Marks, published in *The Old Testament Library* (Philadelphia: Westminster Press, 1961).

indicates that the Hexateuch has had a lengthy tradition-history, but at its base is a comparatively simple, straightforward confessional account of the great acts of God (*magnalia Dei*), beginning with creation and continuing with the call and promises to Abraham, repeated to each patriarchal generation, the deliverance from Egyptian slavery, and the gift of a goodly land. Isolating certain cultic confessions of faith, von Rad found that Israel's epic traditions of her origins as a people were just a developed form of the cultic confessions. He even formulated the hypothesis that in Israel's first written editions of her epic, the Yahwist in the tenth century B.C. simply borrowed the confession as his primary theme, fleshing it out with the inclusion of the Sinai tradition, the development of the Patriarchal history, and the addition of the Primeval History. Essential features of this last hypothesis have since been given up,[12] but von Rad's case remains: Israel's epic tradition in both prose and poetry is a confessional history.

For theology, then, this means that Israel's way was to collect and preserve her historical and prehistorical traditions because the telling of them in different forms and situations related *credo* specifically to current event. Prophets, historians, psalmists, and wise men—none of them can be understood entirely by themselves, apart from the confessional epic continually made relevant to contemporary life. The wisdom literature is generally considered an exception, but it too draws on the epic confessional in the themes employed in the noncultic or wisdom Psalms.[13] This, then, is the primary feature of Israel's life in faith, one made especially clear

[12] They have been given up as a result of Martin Noth's critique: We cannot be so confident that the Yahwist was the real creator of the epic in von Rad's sense because both early editions of the epic (J and E) are so similar that they presuppose a basic *Grundschrift* in oral or written form during the period of the tribal league. Thus von Rad writes in the Foreword to the English tr. of the monograph that it "should now be read in conjunction with Martin Noth's more recent *Überlieferungsgeschichte des Pentateuchs*" (Stuttgart: Kohlhammer Verlag, 1948).

[13] For the designation see S. Mowinckel, "Psalms and Wisdom," *Wisdom in Israel and in the Ancient Near East (Supplements to Vetus Testamentum,* Vol. III; Leiden: E. J. Brill, 1955), pp. 205–244.

when the student approaches it from the perspective of world religions. Israel's creative events were events in time and place, which were celebrated in worship in a great variety of ways. History was not done away with but taken up into worship because God's revelation is in historical action, in events selected as especially "newsworthy" for what they reveal. Around them the sacred literature took form. Teachings, ritual, and oracles are present in abundance, but they receive their context in and are secondary to the special events, the historical tradition.

As revelation the Biblical event was a happening in time deemed of special importance because God's work was present within it, interpreting its meaning. The historical happening and its interpretation, the deed and the word of God as its commentary, these constitute the Biblical event. The centrality of events, furthermore, furnishes the particular Biblical mode by which the knowledge of God is conveyed. An event is expressed by means of a subject conjugating a verb. Neither the subject nor the verb will be analyzed as an entity in itself; the subject realizes itself through the verb, giving the verb its tense, its time.[14] Since in the Bible God is the subject, there is no attempt to penetrate what he is in himself. There is only the testimony to what he has done, together with the body of "inferences" or assumptions that can be deduced from the events. A happening may be charged with meaning. The event may have, as it were, a semantic field around it containing an inexhaustible source of energy as worshipers recall it in their own particular historical situations. Thus the Exodus is recalled in a variety of ways, depending on one's situation. The event as deliverance can be used to point to the power and glory of God as the ground for praise. It can be seen as the portrayal of the righteousness of God, which is the ground of present hope. It shows the content of God's grace as ultimate power reaching into history to save the weak, the poor, the lost; the worshipers are reminded that they are the poor and needy and only as such will they enter the kingdom (Matt. 5:3). The event is also narrated in such a way as to contrast the grace of God with the faithlessness of his people and thus to trans-

---

[14] So Henry Corbin, *Man in Time* (Papers from Eranos Yearbooks; New York, Pantheon Books, 1957), pp. xv–xvi.

form sin into guilt, or betrayal of relationship. People in any variety of circumstances can rehearse the formative event and deduce from it the word of God in their own situation.

In other words, the event-centered mode of God's revelation cannot be systematized, for it includes both the confessional recital of God's activity and the inferences and deductions that a worshiping community draw from it in their own historical situations.

As a phenomenon the Biblical manner of revealing truth has frequently been contrasted in our time with the Greek mode,[15] which has provided the style of classic Christian theology. Such a style rests on a view of reality as a permanent, rational structure, which is not in perpetual movement as is the rush of human events. Here the basic categories for faith are nouns whose semantic "fields" have their reference in the unmoving rational structure. One seeks here the unchanging unities behind the world of change, unities that can be expressed as abstractions, as universals related to one another by the processes of logic. Universals are not declined; they are not in historical movement; they are defined and related to one another as nouns and adjectives, chiefly by the copula "is." What happens in this atmosphere is illustrated by the noun "faith." In most instances in the New Testament it bears the same connotation as in the Old Testament; it is understood only in relation to a subject acting in a manner that can be described as "faithful," which in turn elicits "faith" from the object of the

[15] See, e.g., T. Boman, *Hebrew Thought Compared with Greek* (tr. by J. L. Moreau; Philadelphia: Westminster Press, 1960). James Barr has attempted a critique of this book and other comparable literature in *The Semantics of Biblical Language* (New York: Oxford University Press, 1961), a justified protest against all sorts of extreme statements in the field of Biblical theology. Unfortunately, however, the book does little for the cause it seeks to serve because it timidly avoids a positive analysis of the problem, using "linguistics" as something to step behind when a positive statement is called for. Most unsatisfactory is his treatment of certain weak points in the *Theologisches Wörterbuch zum Neuen Testament* (ed. by Kittel and Friedrich), from which wide generalizations are suggested regarding all lexical attempts in Biblical theology. Any positive discussion was avoided of why dictionaries are necessary and of the role of words as the bearers of semantic "fields" of meaning.

action. In 1 Timothy 6, for example, this is the connotation in verse 11, while in verse 21 it is used as a noun for the "Christian faith" as opposed to current apostasy. Two uses of the term are now present in Christian theology and piety. The more vivid is the post-Reformation usage, "confession of faith," which meant a statement of doctrine to receive intellectual assent, something that has little warrant in the Biblical sense of reality and in the language appropriate to its elucidation.[16]

II

It may be of interest at this point to remark that James Barr in a recent book, *Old and New in Interpretation,* uses the first three chapters to deny the legitimacy of the position just described.[17]

In the first chapter Barr's main point seems to be made: Because of "the multiplex nature of the Old Testament tradition," there is no "single conception which will be adequate to state the character of the tradition. Thus, there is no central motif which will act as the 'key' in the process of understanding." This is especially true with regard to the "acts of God in history," which as a conceptual organizing element "will not work either descriptively or historically." If one were to look at "the actual form of the documents" as they stand, "we have to give space also to all sorts of elements other than these 'acts.' Particular emphasis would have to be given to the speaking of God. . . . We also have to speak of the thinking of Israel and its wise men, of the praises of Israel in its worship, and so on. Only by improbable and forcible apologetics can these be made to 'derive' from an act of God in history. . . ." Further-

[16] The paragraphs are taken from my article "Reflections Concerning Old Testament Theology," *Studia Biblica et Semitica, T. H. Vriesen Dedicata* (Wageningen, Holland, 1966), pp. 382–384.

[17] New York: Harper & Row, 1966. The first and third chapters are an elaboration of Professor Barr's inaugural address as professor at Princeton Theological Seminary (he is now at the University of Manchester): "Revelation through History in the Old Testament and in Modern Theology," *Interpretation,* Vol. XVII (1963), pp. 193–205, reprinted in Martin E. Marty, ed., *New Theology,* No. I (New York: The Macmillan Company, 1964).

more, the more one examines the diversity of tradition, the more one has to question the severe ambiguity of the use of the term "history" in this connection. "The 'historical' acts of God make sense only because they are set within a framework of conceptions, stories, conversations which cannot be expressed by any normal use of the term 'history.' . . . Is there any 'starting-point' for the understanding of the Old Testament? Insofar as the question is a real one at all, the only answer must be the creation story," though even this cannot be used as "the vantage point from which we must see the Bible" because of the latter's multiplicity.

All of this is true from one point of view, and is recognized by all scholars as true. Yet its peculiarity is that it misses almost entirely the point of the scholarly work in modern Biblical theology.

On the one hand, it omits any consideration of the scholarly reasons behind the whole modern effort, begun in Germany, to understand the tradition-history of the "historical books" of the Old Testament and the relation of prophets, psalmists, and wise men to it. Is von Rad entirely mistaken when he argues that what gives outline and what holds together the vast variety of materials in the Hexateuch is the kerygma or *"heilsgeschichtliche* credo"? Is Martin Noth entirely mistaken in his attempt to show that the Deuteronomist's history of Israel in the Promised Land (Deut. to 2 Kings) has an overall theological unity in spite of the complexity of the material it contains? And I would add that the basic elements of that theology are an advanced reflection on the "hexateuchal" credo and covenants.

On the other hand, Barr seems unaware of the real reasons behind the work in comparative religion, singling out historical consciousness as the chief characterizing element of Israel or the Bible in the world of differing religious forms. I first became aware of this from personal conversations with the late Henri Frankfort, from his work, and from continuing contact with perhaps the world's leading theologian of polytheism, Thorkild Jacobsen. One could mention also Mircea Eliade's *The Myth of the Eternal Return* (dealing with the creation theme comparatively, and the reasons for the polytheist's and the Israelite's differing conceptions— an argument that does not fit at all with Barr's mention of the subject in the quotation above), E. Voegelin's *Israel and Revelation,* or even H. Gunkel's understanding of Israel's world view in comparison with the Babylonian world of myth, e.g., in his *The Legends of Genesis.* In the light of such basic work, Barr's hastily and loosely stated reactions to current emphasis on divine activity in history and on the nature of revelation by event simply will not do. The point is not that God speaks as well as acts in the Old Testament, but instead that the two are interrelated. A Biblical event is not simply a happening in time and space, but one in which the word of God is present (the "speaking" of God), interpreting it and giving it special significance.

More important is the question that Barr raises but does not answer. How does the historian handle the vast multiplicity, often contradictory, even chaotic, of any historical movement? He does it by attempting to distinguish and to articulate certain broad or basic characteristics of the movement that seem to hold it together for the most part, so that variety, ambiguity, even contradiction can be dealt with in context. Variety in relation to what, ambiguous in what context, contradictory to what? In the seeming chaos of American religious history, are there not certain basic characteristics which determine it as American, not British or European —and obviously not Indian? Simply to state "the multiplex nature of the Old Testament tradition" is to repeat the obvious, and as a protest against current efforts to handle the peculiar nature of Israelite religiosity the statement fails to make any serious effort to handle the historian's problem.

In the second chapter the author returns to the modern effort to distinguish between Israelite and Hellenic world view, which he began in his *Semantics.*[18] Here again one can agree with most of what is said. Yet the tone of the whole treatment is dominated by protest. The author concentrates on what others have said, and not on the problem in the materials themselves. Again he avoids the historian's task and responsibility.

Barr's third chapter is a "spanking" delivered to all those who

[18] See n. 15.

have considered the Bible as revelation through history, and a protest against Pannenberg's claim that "history is the most comprehensive horizon of Christian theology."[19] Here again, the obvious content of the protest is the ambiguity of the word "history"—is it real history, the idea of history, or what?—and the fact that so much of the Old Testament (many psalms and the wisdom literature) has little to do with history whatever the term means. Indeed, since there is no technical revelational language in the Old Testament (does there *have* to be a *technical* language?—a very problematic position), all theologies in which revelation is "a central and normative concept" are in trouble, especially that of Karl Barth. There are the problems introduced by historical criticism, by attempts to oppose revelation and religion, and by the fact that most revelational models turn out to be Christocentric, "a ceaseless source of embarrassment for the Christian interpreter of the Old Testament. He is expected to interpret the Old Testament with an eye to revelation, and revelation is defined as more or less identical with Christ."

Again, while applauding much of what is said, especially the last point, one is concerned about where we are after the critique is completed. Just because the viewpoint being attacked is full of difficulties and inadequacies does not necessarily mean that it is entirely wrong. Can a more adequate hypothesis be constructed to answer these questions? Would not a Barthian find the author's positive proposals (pp. 100–102), after such a massive critique, pitifully weak? He ends by saying that he is not "denying revelation," but asserting that the variety of Scriptural materials, when recognized, will make possible a more balanced exegesis of the whole than is provided by the concept of history, or by revelation in acts of God, or by Barth's "object-centered" interpretative principle, or by assuming "history" to be the sole theologically unitary

[19] These remarks are only slightly revised from my review in *Interpretation*, Vol. XXII.1 (Jan., 1968), pp. 83–89. For a similar assessment of Barr, with a helpful review of the subject, see E. Cyril Blackman, "Is History Irrelevant for the Christian Kerygma?" *Ibid.*, Vol. XXI.4 (Oct., 1967), pp. 435–446.

concept. I can see little more here than a hope to do better ("We would hope to give more . . ." p. 102). In this hope we can all join! Thus we are left precisely where we were before the book appeared.

III

If Barr's critique leaves us approximately where we started, we are now free to make further queries about the nature of Old Testament theology. The problem with the viewpoint thus far defended is the tension between our desire for theology and an event-studded history in rapid movement. How does one become the other? How does history become theology and theology history?[20]

Von Rad stresses the following points in his conception of the subject matter of Old Testament theology:

First, "It is simply Israel's own explicit assertions about Jahweh . . . with what Israel herself testified concerning Jahweh."[21] The theologian must *not* be primarily concerned with Israel's world of faith, nor with the spiritual and religious realm of Israel. Of course, the abundant witness to Yahweh and to his relationship to Israel and the world should make it possible to draw together "a tolerably complete picture of the religion of the people of Israel" and, with the aid of comparative religion, to point to special features in her conception of God, the distinctiveness of her conceptions of sin and salvation, how God relates himself to the world, etc.

Yet this sort of work, says von Rad, falls within the general study of religion, and it is fitting that at various times orientalists, ethnologists, and students of mythology have cooperated in this type of survey. But this is not the subject matter of Old Testament theology.

[20] This aspect of the subject goes far beyond the question of the relevance of history for theology (cf. Blackman, noted in n. 19). It is the question how they can be the *same*. Note, e.g., such current books as W. Pannenberg *el al., Offenbarung als Geschichte* (Göttingen: Vandenhoeck & Ruprecht, 1961), and a comparable volume in English ed. by J. M. Robinson and J. B. Cobb, Jr., *Theology as History (New Frontiers in Theology,* Vol. III; New York: Harper & Row, 1967).

[21] *Theology of the Old Testament*, Vol. I (see n. 2), p. 105.

Israel's overriding theological concern is much more restrictive. It is confined to the way Israel's writings represented Yahweh's "relationship to Israel and the world in one aspect only, namely as a continuing divine activity in history. This implies that in principle Israel's faith is grounded in a theology of history. It regards itself as based upon historical acts, and as shaped and reshaped by factors in which it saw the hand of Jahweh at work. . . . Even where this reference to divine facts in history is not immediately apparent, as for example in some of the Psalms, it is, however, present by implication: and where it is actually absent, as for example in the Book of Job and in Ecclesiastes, this very lack is closely connected with the grave affliction which is the theme of both these works."[22]

The chief concern must be with what Israel regarded as divine acts in history, with the picture of the divine saving history, which is pronouncedly confessional in character and always filled with the emotions of glorification or regret. "It is this world made up of testimonies that is above all the subject of a theology of the Old Testament."

Second, there is no schematic or systematic unity to Israel's religious viewpoint. The separate acts of revelation are different in content, without an apparent center to hold them together. Von Rad explains: "We can only describe the Old Testament's revelation as a number of distinct and heterogeneous revelatory acts. . . . From first to last Israel manifestly takes as her starting-point the absolute priority in theology of event over 'logos.' . . . Hebrew thinking is thinking in historical traditions. . . . The most varied traditions are superimposed upon one another, and even interwoven. . . ." Individual texts as well as the larger collections "preserve the character of historical documents." The Hexateuch, the Deuteronomist's history of Israel, the Chronicler's history of Judah—all three present their material as history and they all preserve the documentary and confessional character of their oldest components. Their singularly complex form "is the result of Israel's thinking about herself, a process which was constantly operative in the history. Each generation was faced with the ever-identical yet

[22] *Ibid.*, p. 106.

ever-new task of understanding itself as Israel. . . . In this process of actualization the tradition here and there had to be reshaped. . . . No generation produced a perfectly independent and finished historical work—each continued to work on what had been handed down to it. . . . If we cannot divorce Israel's theological world of thought from her world of history . . . , we must beware of striving to reconstruct links between ideas, and systematic combinations, where Israel herself never saw or distinguished such things."[23]

Third, a new dimension in outlook was brought into being by the prophets, who in von Rad's view "expelled Israel from the safety of the old saving actions and suddenly shifted the basis of salvation to a future action of God."[24] Thus an openness regarding the future is a central characteristic of the Old Testament. Israel was always being driven forward by Yahweh's "promises to constant new moments of fulfillment." The unity of the Old Testament is thus not in itself; unlike the New Testament it has no focal point. The unity can only be fulfillment, which is beyond the Old Testament itself. In this sense von Rad sees the New Testament as the goal and fulfillment toward which the Old Testament is directed; the saving events of Israel's confession are reactualized and reinterpreted, the new saving event of Israel's expectation is understood to be at hand, and as a result both Israel's and the Gentiles' relationship to God is on an entirely new basis.[25]

Implicit in von Rad's presentation is a certain view of the nature of theology, analogous perhaps to the Reformation conception of preaching. The preaching moment, when the word of God is heard afresh, is reactualized in an always new situation, in the moment when the community is renewed as God's people. So the Old Testament faith is in the history-centered actions of God, which created Israel and which at each new juncture of experience need reinterpretation, reactualization. There is no unity in current experience, only faith in the living God, then, now, and in the coming salvation. One therefore looks forward to fulfillment. The unity of experience lies only in eschatological hope. The relation between

[23] *Ibid.,* pp. 115–121.
[24] *Ibid.,* Vol. II, p. 118.
[25] *Ibid.,* pp. 319–335, 357–387.

the Testaments is many-faceted, but fulfillment, reinterpretation, reactualization, remain the central features that make it possible to see Christ as the goal of the Old Testament.[26]

Let us now turn to two appraisals of von Rad's work, with differing understandings of the nature of the theological task.

IV

First is a brief but marvelously precise review by Père Roland de Vaux, Roman Catholicism's greatest Old Testament scholar. His title is fascinating: *"Peut-on Écrire une 'Theologie de l'Ancien Testament'?"*[27]

Père de Vaux stresses two characteristics of von Rad's work. First, the confessional history of Israel is sharply separated from the real history, which the historian reconstructs. Immediately, then, we are in trouble because we are compelled to question whether and in what sense Israel's witness is true. Von Rad sees two diametrically opposed histories: the real history and the "holy history" of Israel's testimonies. His theology of the Old Testament, dealing only with the latter, rests on far too pessimistic and skeptical a foundation. The witness of recent excavations has removed the basis for such skepticism.

> One can now establish that Biblical traditions conserve ancient factual memories about the Patriarchal epoch and about its ethnic and social milieu, that the ancestors of the Israelites were Proto-Arameans, that a part of the tribes sojourned in Egpyt, that they settled in Canaan, at least partially by way of conquest, and there, they passed from a semi-nomadic life to a sedentary life. These are the facts which also were retained in

[26] For further explication and defense of his work following a number of critical reviews, see von Rad's "Offene Fragen im Umkreis einer Theologie des Alten Testaments," *Theologische Literaturzeitung,* Vol. LXXXVIII (1963), cols. 403–416.

[27] "Can one write a 'Theology of the Old Testament'?" *Mélanges Chenu* (Paris: Bibliothèque Thomiste, 1967), pp. 439–449; reprinted in a collection of de Vaux's articles, *Bible et Orient* (Paris: Les Editions du Cerf, 1967), pp. 59–71.

the confession of faith in Deut. 26: "My father was a wandering Aramean who went down into Egypt. . . ." The faith of Israel says that all this was brought forth under the direction of God; the modern historian has neither the right nor the possibility of contradicting it.[28]

Père de Vaux's second main concern is von Rad's conception of theology. For von Rad it is not possible to write of one theology of the Old Testament; there are theologies that vary with era and book. One cannot reduce this luxuriance into a system without arbitrary choice, which sacrifices everything that makes each testimony so original. Hence each tradition must be studied for itself. First the historical traditions, to which the Psalms and the wisdom writings are appended as Israel's response—an appending that de Vaux considers somewhat loose (un peu lâche). Then in the second volume the prophetic traditions. No unity in all this can be studied other than what Israel herself perceived. At each moment of its history Israel is conscious of the movement between God's promises and their realization. If the study of Israel's reactualization of divine promise does not continue into the New Testament's witness of Evangelists and Apostles, then in von Rad's view it remains simply a history of the religion of the Old Testament. And that, says de Vaux, is precisely what von Rad gives us—no more. His work is *not* a theology of the Old Testament, but solely a history of Israel's witness, that is, a history of Old Testament religion.[29]

What is de Vaux's basis for this judgment? Von Rad has written a history of how Israel interpreted her past in relation to each present. This is not theology, and such a history is not turned into theology just because it is carried to the threshold of the New Testament. Why? Because, says de Vaux, "theology is the science of faith, not solely by its material object but by the light under which it works. *Fides quaerens intellectum.* . . . As a Christian theologian I receive the Old Testament as the Word of God, the word of *my* God." The theologian searches the rationale of *his* faith, guided by what *his* faith gives him. Von Rad's "holy history"

[28] *Bible et Orient,* pp. 61–64, 67.
[29] *Ibid.,* p. 65.

is not true history; it is a changing interpretation, one often *false,* according to von Rad, of the events of history. Actually, says de Vaux, the unity of the Bible is to be found in the divine plan and revelation. The discovery of this unity is the task of the theologian. "The opposition between Biblical theology and dogmatic theology must disappear." The task of Biblical theology is to search the word of God in order to approach the truth of God.[30] That is, theology is concerned with the truth of God for my tradition, for me.

This understanding of theology as what by knowledge and faith I accept as true recalls Otto Eissfeldt's programmatic article in 1926, which distinguishes the history of Biblical religion from Biblical theology, the difference between the uses of reason and historical method on the one hand, and the methods of faith on the other.[31] Biblical theology is the believer's work, what a member of a particular confession sees as true in the Bible. This recalls also Millar Burrow's dictum that "Biblical theology must package the foods for the consumer" in the churches.[32] T. C. Vriezen in *An Outline of Old Testament Theology,*[33] like de Vaux, protests any purely phenomenological approach to the data because such an approach is not "theological." Moving much further in the same direction, Brevard S. Childs[34] argues that the responsible exegete must begin within "a framework of faith," which for the Christian is defined by and in Jesus Christ. If one begins with the descriptive task and then attempts to establish a bridge to the theological—and this is precisely what most of us who are historical scholars have at-

---

[30] *Ibid.,* pp. 66 and 71.

[31] "Israelitisch-judische Religionsgeschichte und Alttestamentliche Theologie," *Zeitschrift für die alttestamentliche Wissenschaft,* Vol. XLIV (1926), pp. 1–12.

[32] *Journal of Bible and Religion,* Vol. XIV.1 (Feb., 1946), p. 13; cf. his *An Outline of Biblical Theology* (Philadelphia: Westminster Press, 1946).

[33] Wageningen, Holland: H. Vreeman & Zonen, and Chas. T. Banford Co., Newton Centre, Mass. (1958), from the 2nd Dutch ed. (1954), esp. pp. 118–125.

[34] "Interpretation in Faith," *Interpretation,* Vol. XVIII (1964), pp. 432–449.

tempted to do—then, as Childs puts it, "the possibility of genuine theological exegesis has been destroyed from the outset." Childs continues by claiming the descriptive task to be "neutral criticism," which defines in advance the nature of Biblical reality.

De Vaux does not hold that historical exegesis as "neutral criticism" is in oppostion to exegesis in faith. To him the Biblical scholar must operate at various levels, one of which must be historical and descriptive. The two men appear in agreement, however, in thinking of Biblical theology as a study within "a framework of faith," my faith.

With such a conception of theology, we are not only far removed from von Rad's position, we are forced to the conclusion that no one can really write a theology of any religion other than his own. Theology is only about those conceptions with which I personally must deal because my own faith is involved. Here is a problem. Do not other religions have theologies? Is the scholar's attempt to depict them only the history of religion and never theology? The position that subjectivity excludes honest descriptive work of another theology suggests that I as a human being can never penetrate a faith I do not share. Yet to describe the theological views of another is surely theology. It is not simply a general study of religion (von Rad) nor is its particularity exhausted by calling it "history of religion" (de Vaux).[35]

Von Rad's and de Vaux's conceptions of Biblical theology are controlled by their conceptions of what theology is. It must be pointed out, of course, that von Rad believes he is being objective and purely descriptive, but one would be remiss if he failed to point to cultural conditioning, particularly to the variety of tendencies in

[35] Cf. such a work as that of Wilfred Cantwell Smith, *The Meaning and End of Religion* (New York: Mentor Books, 1964), where the contention is that the major religious figures have never preached a "religion." Every "religion" is a channel through which a man of faith finds spiritual transcendence mediated. Thus one cannot depict another "religion" solely by descriptive and historical means. One must penetrate the inner faith and the dynamic inner life of others. Whoever we are with our mundane labels, we are people encountering and responding to life itself.

contemporary German Lutheran theology and the history of the exploration of *heilsgeschichte* in German Biblical studies.

V

For still another view of theology, opposed to both the others, and for a second critique of von Rad's *Theology of the Old Testament,* we turn to the views of Walter Eichrodt. In an Excursus to the English translation of Eichrodt's own *Theology* (see n. 1), he presents an essay on von Rad's work and a partial defense of his own position. After all, he has been under severe German attack for years. Von Rad refers to Eichrodt frequently, but at the outset he has explicitly said:

> Because Old Testament theology took as its task the construction of a history of piety and of the contents of consciousness, and because, above all, it thereby kept to that which has its growth from nature and history, it dismissed what the Old Testament itself had to say, and leaving this aside, chose its own subject of interest for itself.[36]

In spite of Eichrodt's attempt to reevaluate the discipline, von Rad still considers the Swiss scholar's vast effort as included in the general study of religion, not theology. He writes: "I none the less mean to show that even here Old Testament theology has still not yet completely envisaged its proper subject."[37]

Eichrodt responds with all the fervor of a descendant of the Swiss Reformed tradition. How on earth can there be a theology of testimonies about faith-events without any formal structure? Is theology solely a confession of God's acts and a reactualization and reinterpretation in successive historical moments? Who is it that is making the confession and interpretation? Why a people? Why are they a distinctive element in history with their historical *credo*?

Eichrodt starts at this point. What makes this people what they are? The broadest and most penetrating Biblical term for it is

[36] Von Rad, *Theology of the Old Testament,* Vol. I, p. 114.
[37] *Ibid.,* n. 13.

"covenant." He defines it in the broadest context as the way God relates himself to a people, reveals himself as their God, whose will determines the nature of obligation, whose revelation has a factual nature and assumes an interior attitude toward history.

> How deeply this attitude toward history was rooted in the fundamental events of the Mosaic era is shown by the part which the deliverance from Egypt and the occupation of the Holy Land play as a sort of paradigm of the divine succour, not only in the history books, but also in the prophets and the law. Hence it is the ideas of election and the covenant and, closely associated with them, the divine law-giving which become the decisive motifs of the Israelite view of history.[38]

Eichrodt's first strong objection to the label "theology" attached to von Rad's work is the same as de Vaux's. The discrepancy between the reconstruction of Israel's early history and the salvation-history of Old Testament confession wrenches the two apart, so that it is impossible to restore any inner coherence to the two aspects of Israel's history. Accept von Rad's position and Old Testament theology will have to be divorced completely from historical-critical work. If the whole Moses tradition is to be disintegrated, then any conceivable "historical origin for the Yahweh faith is lacking completely." Yahwism as the most vigorous and creative movement in its environment, so distinctive that even von Rad cannot call it into question, "must be ascribed to the chance coalescence of religious ideas springing up here and there—a phenomenon without parallel in religious history." When religious testimony is separated so completely from historical reality, there is little meaning left in any claim for the Bible as "historical revelation." Despite its apparent historical form, Eichrodt claims, if the form has no connection with historical reality, then the religion has to be characterized as a "religious philosophy." All of this is simply part and parcel of a dominant scholarly climate in Germany, of which the theology of Rudolf Bultmann is the chief example.[39]

[38] Eichrodt, *Theology,* Vol. I, p. 42.
[39] *Ibid.,* pp. 512–514. A similar evaluation led Eric Voegelin to argue that "Bultmann's essay on the theological irrelevance of the Old

Eichrodt's second concern is that in von Rad's work it is impossible to present the phenomenon of Israel; there is no self-contained system of belief. "The subject of theological study is not the people of God, held together through all the vagaries of the ages by the continuous exercise of divine love, but a selection of theologically important confessions of faith." If one tries to do more than simply describe the content of these confessions—namely, to expound their particularity and "organic coherence by means of a systemic presentation of Israelite belief"—he is told that this is a dangerous process that can only lead to "bloodless schemata" of religious concepts.[40] In other words, von Rad seems to Eichrodt to characterize the latter's work as "bloodless schemata" of religious concepts, belonging to the study of religion, but not to Old Testament theology.

In the third place, Eichrodt believes that it is all of a piece with von Rad's approach that the relation between the Testaments be conceived as typology, even though strict limitations are placed on its use. Eichrodt writes:

> The discontinuity of the divine revelations which came to Israel, each historically isolated from the others in a way no intellectual religious connection could hope to bridge, points to the fact that these un-cohesive "divine events in history" acquire their ultimate meaning only as forefigurations of the Christ-event. For all this, however, they are to be understood in no instance in their "static givenness" or mere factuality, but in the distinctive "leaning" of their occurrence toward a future fulfillment (II, p. 384). Not that there is any method of confirming or establishing this interpretation (II, p. 387) . . . there is no absolute norm for the Christian understanding of the Old Testament. . . . We must therefore give up all idea of a normative interpretation of the Old Testament, and leave everything to the eclectic charismatic freedom of the

Testament for the Christian faith" has at its core a modern kind of Gnosticism; see B. W. Anderson, ed., *The Old Testament and Christian Faith* (New York: Harper & Row, 1963), pp. 64–89.

[40] Eichrodt, *Theology,* Vol. I, p. 514.

expositor, who will constantly be establishing new typological connections between the Testaments in a great variety of ways.[41]

Eichrodt rightly summarizes all of von Rad's answers to the basic questions of Old Testament theology as exclusively existentialist. "If what matters in both the Old and New Testaments is the existential understanding of the professed believer, and not the presuppositions or individual content of his belief, then obviously the relation of his convictions to history becomes immaterial." Eichrodt continues:

The verdict against a systematic presentation of the totality of Israel's faith . . . loses its stringent character, if the variety of the Old Testament testimonies, which must of course be carefully taken into account in its place, is interpreted not as a discontinuity of the revelatory process, but as the result of observing a complex reality from various angles in ways which are in principle concordant one with another. There is in fact no legitimate reason why we should be forbidden to look for an inner agreement in these testimonies of faith which we have so carefully analyzed; and in this agreement, despite great differentiations and internal tensions, certain common basic features emerge which in combination constitute a system of belief which is both unitary in its essential structure and fundamental orientation and also unique in the history of religions. The charge that such a method only arrives at abstraction is not in fact well conceived. . . . We are not concerned with framing . . . a complete all-round "corpus of doctrine" in the form of a consistent and harmonious intellectual structure. Our purpose is to examine the content for faith of a particular relationship with God, a relationship which has always to be seen as a dynamic process, expressing itself in history in many ways, and fluctuating between periods . . . , but which for all that exhibits . . . fundamental features

[41] *Ibid.,* p. 515.

which mark it out from its religious environment as an entity *sui generis.*[42]

VI

Here, then, are three conceptions of what theology is, each put to work in the service of Old Testament exposition. No wonder very different works appear under the title of Old Testament theology! Differing conceptions of theology combine with differing historical reconstructions of early Israel, and I for one see no way of simple harmonization. Each of three ways of "doing" theology has its defense. Hence if one is to work in the field at all, he has to work out his own position. Here all too briefly is the direction in which I have been moving.

By 1950 I had independently come to a position similar to that of von Rad with regard to revelation by event, the interrelation of word, event, and history (see section I of this chapter). In my monograph of lectures, *God Who Acts: Biblical Theology as Recital* (1952), I found von Rad's theological views, so far as they were then published, most stimulating and helpful. However, with the publication of von Rad's *Theology,* I discovered certain differences of viewpoint:

1. While I agree completely with the confessional center of revelation to Israel, it appears that von Rad, like Bultmann,[43] has carried the Lutheran separation of law and gospel back into his Old Testament scholarship so that Israel's recitals of the *magnalia Dei* are interpreted as having nothing to do originally with the Sinai covenant tradition. The welding of the two is a secondary phenomenon, which marked the beginning of the law-gospel tension in the Bible. This viewpoint from a scholarly standpoint has been rendered highly unlikely by George E. Mendenhall's basic work, *Law and Covenant in Israel and the Ancient Near East* (1954–1955), and by the dissertation of one of von Rad's own students, Klaus Baltzer,

---

[42] *Ibid.,* p. 517.

[43] Cf. my analysis in "History and Reality . . . ," Chap. 10 in B. W. Anderson, ed., *The Old Testament and Christian Faith.*

Das Bundesformular (1960),[44] the implications of which von Rad evidently cannot face. The pioneering work of Mendenhall and Baltzer means that the two forms, *magnalia Dei* and Sinai covenant tradition, are inseparable and that the covenant is the setting for the recitation of the acts.

2. This means that Eichrodt is right in insisting that Israel's testimonies find their setting and particularity only in the framework of the Sinai covenant. Von Rad's existentialist interpretation of Israel's theology has no *Sitz im Leben* apart from a people dominated by the conception of a world empire whose Suzerain has created a people, Israel, whose identity is one of vassalage by treaty in the cosmic empire. Hence Old Testament theology without a sense of this cosmic structure, which informs Israel's every testimony, is simply impossible.[45]

3. What, then, is theology? I must side with Eichrodt that it is impossible to separate testimonies to God's saving activity, reactualized in succeeding periods, from conceptual and structural elements provided by the Sinai covenant tradition. On the other hand, Eichrodt is much too wedded to older terms like "system," "systematic," which are unnecessary. "Coherence" and *sui generis* seem to me more appropriate.

In other words, theology is the effort of a man to explicate his own or someone else's tradition meaningfully in his conceptual world, so that he can understand it. To restrict theology to the proclamation of Israel's or the Christian's kerygma is too confining. What is kerygma without exposition and application? What is

[44] Mendenhall's work originally appeared as Vol. XVII.2 and 3 (May and Sept., 1954) of *The Biblical Archaeologist,* and reprinted as a monograph in 1955 from the same plates. It is now available from the Presbyterian Board of Colportage, 215 Oliver Avenue, Pittsburgh, Pa. 41222. The Baltzer volume was published by Neukirchen Verlag in Neukirchen-Vluyen, Germany.

[45] For a proper discussion of the political form of the Bible, which so many today want to "demythologize," see, e.g., Paul Lehmann, *Ethics in a Christian Context* (New York: Harper & Row, 1963), Chap. III, entitled "What God is Doing in the World."

the proclamation of the Word apart from the structure of "the people of God" whom it has created and whom it recreates?

On the other hand, a preoccupation with a "system of belief" may miss the point. This places too much emphasis on man the thinker, on theology as the rational content of faith. The logic of the individual thinker can no longer be considered the key to either existence or Reality.[46] One thing fairly common to the many varieties of existentialism today is the rejection of the whole epistemological trend of philosophy and theology that began with Descartes, the tendency to separate the knower from the known. Today the opposite tendency, as I understand it, is to define the human being, not simply by his individuality in and for itself, but by the whole environmental and historical nexus by which he has been formed and in which he now lives.

From medieval psychology on it has been a common thing to say that amidst all the individual variation, one thing we can count on is that human nature is always the same. Yet this long-held assumption can and should be challenged.[47] To be sure, our biological structure as members of the species Homo sapiens is constant and this permits a great deal of generalization about human beings, but it also permits vast variety and almost limitless possibilities. We have inherited a large variety of psychophysical tendencies; we have been produced in different families with their differing traditions and interests; our societies, educations, and friendships all differ; and our vocational choices have brought new vistas, new varieties and determinants for the questions: Who am I? Who was I? What will I become? I cannot be known simply by the applications of psychologist, sociologist, or anthropologist. I am an individual with a history not entirely predetermined by genes or environment. I am a creature of choices, a bundle of biases in my past and present

[46] For a strong statement in this vein, see Joseph Haroutunian, *God with Us: A Theology of Transpersonal Life* (Philadelphia: Westminster Press, 1965).

[47] See the very creative article by Gordon D. Kaufman, "The *Imago Dei* as Man's Historicity," *Journal of Religion,* Vol. 36 (1956), pp. 157–168.

relationships with others, with my environment. In other words, what is important to say is that I am a historical being always making choices—or in the words of Joseph Haroutunian, I was made "as a fellow man." Of course, I am a finite creature in space and time with their power structures, but I too possess a power structure with the ability to create what no tradition, no depth psychologist, no environmentalist—no combination of them—can entirely predict.

At this point, the Old Testament presentation of man has been getting a hearing denied by an earlier age, when different views of man prevailed.

For one thing, it is now clear that in the Bible man is a psychophysical organism. This idea corresponds with modern conceptions about the mind-body problem, psychosomatic interrelation, etc. Man as an incarnate soul, in other words, must be rejected, and Biblical materials can successfully be used in this environment[48]

Second, the cliché that "one man is no man" applies very well to Biblical conceptions of man and society and what has been affirmed above[49]

Third, man discovers himself *and* his insights, not simply by thought, but by action and interaction, by fellowship with other men in situations that cause challenge and response, advance and retreat, the choice of alternatives, and the constant necessity of new decisions in the face of new situations, new demands and pressures, new people. Thus there is no insight in isolation. Theology cannot be simply thoughts; it must be a structure of involvement and decision-making in which insight, knowledge, and ideas have an active and reactive context.

Still another point that might be mentioned in the Biblical presentation of man is that he was created for light and not for darkness—a basic issue in both the Old and New Testaments, for which

[48] For a bit of bibliography here, see Walter Eichrodt, *Man in the Old Testament* (*Studies in Biblical Theology*, No. 4, 1951); John A. T. Robinson, *The Body—A Study in Pauline Theology* (*ibid.*, No. 5, 1952); H. Wheeler Robinson, *Inspiration and Revelation in the Old Testament* (New York: Oxford University Press, 1946).

[49] Cf. my *The Biblical Doctrine of Man in Society* (London: SCM Press, 1954).

a text might be John 3:19–21. In the rich symbolism of those terms for both Biblical and modern man, we are again directed toward active, creative involvement of man in his nexus if we are to understand him.

From this perspective, one might conclude that von Rad's theological viewpoint is more in keeping with the flexibilities, complexities, and situation-centered context of thought and decision. Yet the question intrudes whether he has sufficiently explored the socioenvironmental context of Israel's "testimonies" and statements about God and herself. Israel lived in a world structured by basic symbols consciously accepted or borrowed from her environment, while others were consciously rejected as inappropriate. Those accepted generally played different roles in the new environment or were reinterpreted.

The reason for these obvious examples from current Biblical study is not the kind of blind bibliolatry which assumes that anything Biblical is automatically useful in our day. They are given here because they are instructive. They are features of the Biblical mode of viewing reality now seen to have a fresh and instructive word for us in our time. The world changes; suppositions once taken for granted die away. Suddenly we can hear fresh voices in the Bible because our hearing "improves," or at least is altered. That is, the "field" in which we live changes and we change with it. And surely the doctrine of the Spirit means that in such a case "from now on I make you hear new things, hidden things which you have not known" (Isa. 48:6).

In any event, from both the modern and Biblical ways of viewing man, thought has both a biological and an environmental nexus. Structural elements are clearly involved; the problem is to recognize and to analyze them. And since both our biological and environmental contexts are rarely static, the structures of thought require fresh interpretation. Theologically, the content we put into the word "God," for example, requires continued updating, as does our style of thinking and speaking about revelation or about the Trinity or about Christology. No theology can remain static. No system of thinking articulated in a particular time can be considered unchangeable. It becomes dated as events and people change. In the new environment old issues must be discussed anew.

From such a perspective, is not von Rad correct? Each age must indeed interpret older religious assertions anew—this is precisely von Rad's view of theology. Yet can one neglect so competely the structural norms? On the whole, while Eichrodt's work is badly in need of recasting in line with the work done since the 1930's, I find his view of the theological task much broader and more satisfying. Old Testament theology is something more than a scholar's résumé in modern terms of Israel's explicit statements about God and what he has done, and what Israel and the peoples of the world have done, will experience, or can hope. It is also a reflection on the meaning and implications of those statements as a "style" of religious expression amidst the world of differing religious possibilities. Only to the extent that this is true can one be sure of what he means or what Israel meant when Biblical words are repeated. The dangers are those of any historical enterprise—misinterpreting, failure of proper generalization, empathy for historical particularity, etc.

The implications for the question "What is theology?" are equally difficult to state. I am certain in my own mind that theology is not "the rational content of faith." It is first and foremost a human *activity*, which deals with basic issues of intrapersonal and transpersonal life in this world where past, present, and future are ambiguous and dangerous, yet exciting, full of drama and full of hope. It is a searching for God as he has been and is relating himself to us in our specific time and place. It is an activity that demands and is continual conversation with one's peers, past and present. Theological activity is reasoning, reflective, interpretative, seeking those vital structures of meaning that hold life together, that release our freedom and power for creativity; it avoids the systems that have so busily translated "the language of faith into a body of inert terminology."[50] Finally, theology is an action and reaction of

---

[50] See Joseph Haroutunian, *First Essay in Reflective Theology* (Inaugural Address as Cyrus H. McCormick Professor of Theology), *McCormick Seminary Addresses,* No. III, 1943), p. 520.

people together in history who have a history and a complex historical language through which they think, feel, and communicate with one another.[51] It does not provide final answers to this or that problem; instead it is the activity that explores the meaning of the human enterprise on earth and, therefore, is the undergirding of all our life together.

The form of revelation in the Bible suggests, when seriously taken, that this is a theology of both thinking about and involvement in the human enterprise on earth, within the structuring norms of a shared community that create one as a person. In the matter of Biblical interpretation, however, the opinion held by me or by my community must be set aside, insofar as possible, at the outset of the theological effort in order that I hear and know what people are saying in an age or context other than my own. There is a long bridge of time and tradition between where we now are and the Biblical periods. Consequently, should I not employ all the tools of the modern linguist and historian to be sure that I understand and interpret aright? If the Bible is the revelation of a new reality in a Near Eastern time and place, why should not the historian's tools be my ally in bridging the gap between the times so that I do not misrepresent and misinterpret? To think of the work of the historian solely as "neutral criticism" with no attempt at empathy or personal involvement is simply not true to the manner in which most historians work. They seek to know the "truth" about the culture they are studying, and to know it from as far inside as they are capable. If I am to describe another's life, such honest historical searching is what is required of me. And when the revelation comes to us in the forms of history, does not that say a great deal about its character? And does that not also say that any heir of the Judeo-Christian heritage, if he would penetrate it, must become something of a historian, not simply for the sake of honesty, but for the sake of faith?

[51] See further Gordon D. Kaufman in n. 47 above; also his *Relativism, Knowledge and Faith* (University of Chicago Press, 1966).

VII   Summary

The area of greatest influence of the Old Testament on modern theology is in its form and style as a mode of revelation. The peculiar intertwining of historical events and traditions with confession leads to the assertion that Israel was the first people in world history to become so interested in preserving in narration her historical traditions. And this was for theological reasons; Israel's God was the Lord of history.

It is only within the last generation that certain theologians have begun to take Israel's event-confessional mode of revelation seriously as the only manner in which the Biblical knowledge of God can be conveyed. This means a different style of theology than has been customary. Yet few have carried this central insight through into a coherent and consistent position. Gerhard von Rad's *Theology of the Old Testament* is the most original effort in the field of Biblical Theology to work along these lines. When this great work is closely examined through the eyes of certain of his critics, however, it becomes very clear that each person, von Rad and each of his critics, is operating with a different conception in his mind as to just what theology is. No wonder, then, that theologies differ so radically!

The discussion finally must turn to the conception of man that is appropriate for our time and then ask what one is doing when he is working theologically. In such a context the history-centered view of man and what that implies come to the foreground. The result is the conception of the theological task in line with the work of Wolfhart Pannenberg[52] in Germany and of Gordon D. Kaufman[53] in the United States, both of whom have envisaged a theology with history

[52] See esp. the programmatic work of the Pannenberg circle in *Offenbarung als Geschichte* (*Kerygma und Dogma,* Beiheft 1; Göttingen: Vanderhoeck und Ruprecht, 1961; 2nd ed., 1963); and James M. Robinson and John B. Cobb, Jr., eds., *Theology as History* (*New Frontiers in Theology,* Vol. III; New York: Harper & Row, 1967).

[53] See esp. Kaufman's *Systematic Theology: A Historicist Perspective* (New York: Charles Scribner's Sons, 1968). This volume appeared

as the central category or as the matrix of all thinking about God and his revelation. While the works of these men are not discussed in the present volume, the reader will note that to carry out the theological task from what has been central to recent Old Testament theology would lead one, in the writer's opinion, in directions being charted by these two men among others.

---

after my manuscript had been completed. Consequently, it is not otherwise cited in this book. I am greatly indebted to my colleague, however, for numerous insights gained from frequent discussions.

3

God the Creator

THE PURPOSE of the next four chapters is briefly to examine certain primary assumptions and assertions about God in the Old Testament which have been basic to the Judeo-Christian heritage. An attempt will be made to suggest some reasons why they still are not unreasonable and why they must be taken seriously by all those who would preserve some connection with the Biblical understanding of reality.

In Genesis 14:19 an old title of El, head of the Canaanite pantheon of gods, is assumed by Israelite editors of the tradition to be an appropriate title of the God of Israel. It is *qōnēh shāmaym wā-'áreṣ,* "Creator of Heaven and Earth."[1] This means that both Israel and polytheist Canaan had conceptions of creation and of a creator-deity. Why should this be so? Other Asian religions east of western Asia seem not to find the doctrine of creation particularly pertinent to the human problem. For them creation is simply foreign to, or at least plays no primary role in, religious faith and action. This suggests that religions which do place creation at a central place in tradition and liturgy are under an inner necessity to do so. That is, a creation story, or a reflection on creation, has a primary role to play in the understanding, not simply of the beginnings of universe, world and life, but most especially of our present-day existence as human beings. A creation story is never for *kinderfrage,* that is for children's questions about how the world began.[2]

---

[1] For setting and background see the important article of Frank M. Cross, Jr., "Yahweh and the God of the Fathers," *Harvard Theological Review,* Vol. LV.4 (Oct., 1962), pp. 222–259.

[2] That is, literary critical scholarship was divided on whether the early Genesis stories were primitive and, therefore, childlike in facing cos-

70

I

During the last quarter century the theologies of ancient poly-theisms have become much better known. And they furnish an excellent illustration of the point just made. The doctrine of creation lies at their very center because of the analysis of the problem of human existence which the religions are attempting to answer. Creation was the all-important concern of everyday life in the streets and fields. The reason was the pervading sense of insecurity. Life was a very fragile thing; its well-being depended so completely on the order and fertility of a natural world that was both predict-able and unpredictable—predictable as a rule, but never entirely dependable because of the ever-frightening storm which in a few minutes could destroy years of work, or because of barrenness and sickness and death.

The great polytheisms of Biblical times were by no means primitive religions, no matter the primitive features which survived within them. They were highly sophisticated analyses of nature. Their gods were the powers who controlled and regulated nature; they were imminent within the order of the world, indeed the very life and power of nature.

Creation, then, took the form of a battle between divine beings which resulted in chaos-monsters being destroyed and the ordered world being established. Everything in heaven and on earth was now fitted into its place and purpose. The overriding concern of life and rite was to keep things that way. Yet there was still un-certainty. Both cosmic and earthly forces of disorder were always a threat to the rhythm of healthy life in the bosom of nature. For this reason official worship was centered in certain dramatic rites, the purpose of which was to maintain the benefits of creation. The original battle was cultically refought yearly during the New Year's celebrations, and its benefits extended to the year ahead. The primordial event was the central and all-important event of exist-

mological issues, or whether in their simplicity they were actually very profound, ence. The sense of movement toward a future was unknown because life was always turning back to the mythical event and re-creating it for security's sake. Mircea Eliade has called it *The Myth of the Eternal Return*.[3] Creation and the maintenance of its benefits was for these religions the single most absorbing concern on which everything else depended.

When we turn to Israel, it is also true that every man desired security, to sit under his vine and his fig tree where none would terrify. He desired a world where the weapons of war would be beaten into agricultural tools, and he desired a Holy Land where "they shall not hurt or destroy" (Isa. 11:9). Yet security was not the Hebrews' chief word. The problem of the world was at a much deeper level. It was the fact that man had refused the conditions of his creation; he had pitted his will against his Creator; this was the basic trouble. As long as man used his will in defiance of the conditions of his creation, there can be no security whatever in this earth.

This is quite a different evaluation of the human problem. Consequently, the meaning of the creation theme was something very different in Israel from what it was in polytheism. Creation was Israel's inferring the conditions of all life and of world order from what was known in the society of the covenant. Man is the ruling lord of all things on earth, but he is also the servant who is responsible to the Creator. The Lord of the covenant is the Creator of the universe, independent of, and not to be confused with, his creation. And the Creator is the Lord who rules his creation. In this one assertion came the beginning of the demythologizing of nature, on which our modern western world of history and science rests. The Greeks also were to demyth nature and to turn

[3] *Cosmos and History: The Myth of the Eternal Return* (tr. by Willard Trask; New York: Harper & Row, 1954). The best treatment of polytheism theologically is still that of Frankfort, Jacobsen, and Wilson, *The Intellectual Adventure of Ancient Man* (Chicago: University of Chicago Press, 1946; reprinted by and still available from Penguin Books). See also the important volume of Robert C. Dentan, ed., *The Idea of History in the Ancient Near East* (New Haven: Yale University Press, 1955).

the gods into symbols, but they did it by asserting the supremacy of reason over myth. Israel did it by asserting that the world was the creation of the Divine Ruler of the universe. Therefore, the mythologies of the gods of nature were pure fiction, the product of human perversity.

For Israel, as for Babylon and for Canaan, the creation doctrine presented the very conditions of everyday existence, but with what difference of emphasis! And the difference came from another analysis of the meaning of world order and the human problem. Man's will committed and obedient to the Creator-Lord involved a much deeper inner and personal relation between man and his Lord than is customary in the religions of the world. Biblical man learned this from the covenant relation, that most profound of all Biblical relationships. In it he also confronted the mystery of his creation: that only in the trusting and obedient life was his true peace and freedom. Freedom on any other ground is a slavery that can never liberate. Jeremiah says of Israel in God's name:

> I planted you a choice vine,
>   wholly of pure seed.
> How then have you turned degenerate
>   and become a wild vine?
>
> (2:21 RSV)

That is the Bible's correlation of the "death of God" with the degeneration of man. This is the repeated assertion of the prophets, and made equally explicit by the Apostle Paul in Romans 1. Dean F. Thomas Trotter is one among others who have repeatedly made the same assertion in modern times:

> Truly ours is a world in which truth and reality seem to have collapsed into relativity. The "death of God," despite the speculations of Nietzsche and Dostoyevsky, has ushered in, not the age of man, but rather the age of anxiety, alienation, irrationalism, and boredom. Here is, in truth, the "death of man" as a self-conscious and responsible individual.[4]

[4] "Variations on the 'Death of God' Theme in Recent Theology," *Journal of Bible and Religion,* Vol. XXXIII.1 (Jan., 1965), pp. 42–48 (quote from p. 48).

II

Can this Biblical depiction of the conditions of human existence be brought into our modern world and be accepted as true?

We certainly do not need to argue the point that unchanneled freedom leaves a person at the mercy of all those inner irrational forces which Freudian psychology has laid bare. Proper discipline alone is what makes creative freedom a possibility, as any great pianist or golfer knows. Our problem again is whether "God the Creator" is a meaningful or a nonsensical expression.

Let us turn back again to the creation theme in the Old Testament. It is used, beginning as early as the tenth century and the period of David and Solomon in Jerusalem, by three different theological schools: (1) those who committed Israel's epic to writing; (2) the school of wisdom; and (3) the theologians of Jerusalem's Davidic dynasty.

The royal theologians in Jerusalem laid the foundations of the Davidic dynasty in firmer soil than in the problematic and conditional grounds of the Mosaic covenant. In order to make the monarchy palatable at all, Samuel's compromise was to divide the office of "judge" in the Tribal League into two offices, the prophetic which continued the charismatic or Spirit-empowered leadership of the League, and the politico-military function in the person of Saul, whom conservatives could still refer to as *nāgîd,* an old League term, instead of *mélek,* the Canaanite term for king, if they chose (e.g., 1 Sam. 10:1). The new leader ruled by the word of the Lord, and it was the new prophetic office which transmitted the Word.[5]

[5] See my "The Lawsuit of God," *Israel's Prophetic Heritage* (ed. by B. W. Anderson and W. Harrelson; New York: Harper & Row, 1962), pp. 26–27; Lecture 6 on "The Rule of God," *The Rule of God* (New York: Doubleday & Company, 1960), pp. 95–109; "The Nations in Hebrew Prophecy," *Encounter* (Christian Theological Seminary, Indianapolis), Vol. 26 (1965), pp. 225–237; and independently W. F. Albright, *Samuel and the Beginnings of the Prophetic Movement* (The Goldensen Lecture for 1961; Cincinnati: Hebrew Union College Press).

While the tradition placed David in this succession (e.g., 1 Sam. 16:13), royal theologians during the course of the tenth century evolved a different theology for the royal office. This involved God's eternal commitment to the dynasty of David, a commitment as firmly established as God's creation of an ordered world in the midst of chaos, and his choice of Zion as the site of his tabernacle forever. Early psalms in this tradition present the themes from which we can reconstruct something of the theology. God's righteousness as traditionally depicted in the elevation of the poor from the dust is coupled with his creative action and the exaltation of his king: "There is none as holy as Yahweh . . . ; Indeed, a God of knowledge is Yahweh . . . ; He is one who raises the poor from the dust . . . ; Indeed, the pillars of the earth are Yahweh's; on them he has set the world . . . ; He gives strength to his king; he exalts the horn of his anointed" (1 Sam. 2:2, 3, 8, 10). The pre-exilic Psalm 89 speaks of the heavens as erected in Yahweh's eternal loving-kindness (*ḥésed*) and of his eternal covenant with David and his descendants (vss. 2–4). At this point, the Psalmist breaks into a magnificent hymn in praise of the Creator who rules over the Sea, the symbol of ancient chaos, and crushes the chaos-monster Rahab, here no longer merely the symbol of the natural chaos which in creation was slain by the forces of order,[6] but also the symbol of historical enemies whom Yahweh "scattered with thy powerful arm." Righteousness and justice are the foundation of his throne. "Indeed our (royal) shield belongs to Yahweh; our king belongs to the Holy One of Israel" (vss. 5–18; Heb. 6–19).[7]

The wisdom movement could also refer in the language of the

---

[6] A poetic reference to the Canaanite myth of creation, which like the Babylonian involved a theogony in which the chaos-monster, who could also be referred to as Sea, the dragon in the sea, River, or Leviathan, was slain by the chief executive of the pantheon of deities who had been appointed to his office as the warlord for this battle.

[7] We shall return to this royal theology in Chap. 5. For the best current expositions of it, see Bernhard W. Anderson, *Creation vs. Chaos* (New York: Association Press, 1967), esp. Chap. 2 on "Creation and Covenant"; and R. E. Clements, *Prophecy and Covenant* (Studies in Biblical Theology, No. 43; London: SCM Press, Ltd., 1965; Naperville, Ill.: Alec R. Allenson).

Canaanite creation myth to the providential power of God who alone could control the chaos-dragon, though in Job 41 the dragon remains unhistoricized as the symbol of the unruly, chaotic forces of nature. Of special interest, however, is Proverbs 8:22–31 where wisdom is the first of God's creative works and was beside him in the creation of the world. In other words, wisdom, that practical, prudential, moral knowledge of what is best for daily life, is God's creation, which preexists the very foundations of human existence. It cannot be equated in value with anything in the universe (Job 28:12–28); its source is God alone who knows the way to it and who has revealed its rootage to man in the words:

> Behold, the reverence of God, this is wisdom;
> and to turn aside from evil is discernment.
>
> (vs. 28)

This world is created in such a way that man can have confidence that the ethical life is rooted in the very creation itself and derives from God the Creator. While this view furnishes all sorts of problems when one encounters suffering and evil triumphant, as in many psalms, in Job, and in Ecclesiastes, it is nevertheless consistent with what was said in the last chapter about the structure of the self being fulfilled in positive goals, and about man being created for light and not for darkness in the determination of those goals. Ultimately, this is a faith and an eschatological hope which do not resolve earth's contradictions but which nevertheless can furnish the ground upon which present existence is erected.

Of course, wisdom (Sophia in Greek) as the first of God's creative acts will become a very useful conception in later Gnosticism. On the other hand, when during the Exile or postexilic period wisdom is identified with both the law and the word of God,[8]

---

[8] Cf. Ezra 7:14 and 25 where the document in Ezra's possession, presumably the completed Pentateuch, is called both the law and the wisdom of God. The mixing of legal and wisdom forms of speech is particularly clear in the postexilic Ps. 119. It is understanding which one needs in order to learn the law (vss. 34, 73, 125), and I need this understanding to live (vs. 144). It is the word of God which is firmly fixed in the heavens and which is the ground of hoped-for salvation (vss. 89 ff.). The law can even make the simple wise so that it is

a setting is created whereby the same thing can be said about the word of God at the creation as Proverbs 8 claimed for wisdom, and it is this creative word which became flesh in Christ (John 1).

In this chapter, however, special attention is called to the function of the creation stories in Genesis, Second Isaiah and certain of the psalms. The framers of Israel's epic in its canonical form did not view God's act of creating the world as set apart from his other activity. It was simply the first of his series of acts in a time-sequence, mighty acts selected because of their basic nature, but for all of which God is to be praised.[9] A trilogy of lengthy postexilic psalms is indicative of the developed theology of this group; they should not be separated as though they were independent entities. The first, Psalm 104, is a hymn in praise of the Creator:

> Thou didst set the earth on its foundations,
>   so that it should never be shaken. . . .

> From thy lofty abode thou waterest the mountains;
>   the earth is satisfied with the fruit of thy work. . . .

> O Lord, how manifold are thy works!
>   In wisdom hast thou made them all;
>   the earth is full of thy creatures. . . .

---

more desired than gold (Ps. 19:7–10). In other words, since word and wisdom are both known by revelation, the priestly postexilic community understood that they were ultimately related. This was responsible for the preservation of both great legal and wisdom collections and traditions. For fixing of these identities only in a later period see J. Coert Rylaarsdam, *Revelation in Jewish Wisdom Literature* (Chicago: University of Chicago Press, 1946).

[9] See on this point G. von Rad, "The Theological Problem of the Old Testament Doctrine of Creation," *The Problem of the Hexateuch and Other Essays* (tr. by E. W. T. Dicken, New York: McGraw-Hill, 1966), pp. 131–143. Von Rad fails to note that the carriers of the creation theme between the tenth and sixth centuries (between J and Second Isaiah) were Jerusalem's royal theologians. This omission in his stimulating and pioneering article is repaired independently by Anderson, Clements (see n. 7 above), and this author (in "Schöpfung, II. Im AT," *Religion in Geschichte und Gegenwart*, 3rd ed., Vol. V, Tübingen: J. C. B. Mohr [Paul Siebeck], Columns 1473–1477).

> When thou sendest forth thy Spirit, they are created;
> and thou renewest the face of the ground. . . .

> I will sing to the Lord as long as I live;
> I will sing praise to my God while I have being. . . .

> Bless the Lord, O my soul!
> Hallelujah!
>
> (104:5, 13, 24, 30, 33, 35 RSV)

In Psalm 105 the story of the work of God for Israel is rehearsed from Abraham to the gift of the land. And again the psalm ends with "Hallelujah!" Psalm 106 begins and ends with "Hallelujah!" The great works of God for Israel are rehearsed, but this time as a ground for confession. The graciousness of God's actions is the background for the recitation of Israel's faithless acts in response.

It is in Second Isaiah (Chaps. 40–55) that the first primary use of the creation theme in prophecy is to be found. Not only is creation the setting of praise for the Creator, but as in Genesis and in the trilogy of Psalms 104–106 the creative and redemptive acts of God are immediately associated.

> Thus says God, the Lord,
> Who created the heavens and stretched them out,
> Who spread forth the earth and what comes from it,

> Who gives breath to the people upon it
> and spirit to those who walk in it:

> I am the Lord, I have called you in righteousness,
> I have taken you by the hand and kept you;

> I have given you as a covenant to the people,
> a light to the nations,
> to open the eyes that are blind,

> To bring out the prisoners from the dungeon
> from the prison those who sit in darkness.
>
> (42:5–7 RSV)

Second Isaiah in stressing God's creative work is identifying the power on earth which is working universal salvation. His election or appointment of Israel is that of an agent or servant who has a role to play in this mighty activity. Another vigorous passage makes the point even more clear:

> Awake, awake, put on strength,
> O arm of the Lord;
>
> Awake, as in the days of old,
> the generations of long ago.
>
> Was it not thou that didst cut Rahab in pieces,
> that didst pierce the dragon?
>
> Was it not thou that didst dry up the sea,
> the waters of the great deep;
>
> that didst make the depths of the sea a way
> for the redeemed to pass over?
>
> And the ransomed of the Lord shall return,
> and come with singing to Zion;
>
> everlasting joy shall be upon their heads;
> they shall obtain joy and gladness,
> and sorrow and sighing shall flee away.
> (51:9–11 RSV)

Here metaphorical allusion is made to the Canaanite creation myth in which the dragon of chaos is killed that world order may emerge. The God of Israel slew that dragon, but the event is of the same kind as the salvation of Israel at the Red (Reed) Sea, and the salvation, the new Exodus from slavery, that is about to come.

Creation, then, is both the establishment of the conditions of our existence and the release into time and history of that creative power which has worked and is working positively to put the broken together, to heal the sick, and to release the captives.

As von Rad has stressed (see n. 9), the developed kerygmatic confession of Israel simply recites the creation as the first in the series of God's mighty acts, the first event of the *heilsgeschichte* (history of divine salvation). And this is precisely the way the creation stories in Genesis function as the setting of God's creation and choosing of Israel, his salvation of Israel in the Exodus, and his gift of a land in which his people could live. The Genesis creation stories, then, permit the following deductions:

1. The God encountered by Israel as Redeemer is affirmed as the Creator of heaven and earth.

2. The stories of creation will be recounted by Israel as history, even though they represent history's beginning, and they will be related by narrative and genealogy to the period of the Patriarchs or fathers of Israel. They belong, therefore, within time, in contrast to creation myths which lie outside a time framework as the primordial which is always in need of representation for the community's renewal.[10]

3. The creation stories identified man in the creation and explained his role as the ruler of the world (Gen. 1:28). At the same time, it identified the Creator as man's Sovereign Lord to whom he then and now was and is responsible.

4. Creation refers to the power of the Creator to form for man a good world, the fitting setting for the good life under God as Lord—a view which will resist all worldly pessimisms which place evil in the structure of nature.

5. Yet, since man's life in the world is in defiance of the order created for him, history has as central to it the work of God to restore the creation to its condition as originally planned, a good world of peace and order. This will furnish the overall viewpoint in which the rebellions, judgments, and miseries of history will be interpreted.

6. Thus Creator and Savior or Redeemer are one and the same God; and the work of God in creation can be recited as the first of God's mighty acts for which he is to be praised.

7. Because of man's rebellion and the growth of civilization under both God's blessing and his curse, the work of the Creator is

[10] Cf. S. Mowinckel, *Religion und Kultus* (Göttingen: Vandenhoeck & Ruprecht, 1953), as well as Mircea Eliade, *op. cit.* (n. 3).

not yet completed. The same power which brought order from chaos and established man as vicegerent of the earth is to be observed as judging and redeeming power in human history. It is this creative power on which man's hope of earth can rest, hope for a future, hope that present misery and defeat of hope are not eternal, hope by which man dares to see meaning in history.

III

Israel's creation "doctrines" thus start with interpreted experience of past and present. This is true whether the breakdown of the Tribal League leads to the attempt to place the wonders of David's kingship in the setting of the created order, or whether it is wisdom's certainty that the ethical life must have its rootage in the very structure of creation, or whether the Exodus and other *magnalia Dei* reveal that redemptive power in history which must be the same power that created the world and so is to be identified as the world's Lord. That is, there is a deductive aspect to the conception of creation wherein present experienced realities are posited as firmly seated in the created order and in the will of the Creator. As such, then, they are deemed dependable realities upon which future hope can rest.

Can the conception of God as Creator from this perspective play, not only a useful, but an indispensable role in one's own theology in our day? The assumption that God is the Creator of our visible universe was once described by Reinhold Niebuhr as one of the permanent "myths" which belong to the very structure of the Christian religion and to be sharply distinguished from other less essential "myths" of the Bible, which the Church through history has found dispensable.[11] As such, therefore, it is not something subject to proof. Indeed, it can be denied, and the man struggling today for faith cannot oppose his "proofs" and expect them to persuade. Yet, if he can place positive content in the word "God,"

[11] Reinhold Niebuhr, "The Truth in Myths," *The Nature of Religious Experience: Essays in Honor of Douglas Clyde Macintosh* (ed. by J. S. Bixler; New York: Harper & Brothers, 1937), pp. 118–119.

he can make sense out of the doctrine of creation, provided that he can come to an interpretation of history which can reasonably be said to necessitate it or to support it.

The school of modern theology, I am informed,[12] which has placed special stress upon the importance of the creative in human history, is that one, formerly centered in the University of Chicago, which has developed its theology on the philosophical basis provided by Alfred North Whitehead. Its mode of thinking has been characterized usually as "process theology." To obtain the "flavor" of this type of thinking, let us present a few quotations from Henry Nelson Wieman's *The Directive in History*:[13]

> There is a power at work in our midst whereby the thought and feeling of each gets across to the other, whereby this thought and feeling derived from the other is integrated into the mind of each, thus expanding the richness and resources of the mind and personality. This power creates the human

[12] By my colleague, Gordon D. Kaufman.

[13] Boston: The Beacon Press, 1949. Cf. also Bernard E. Meland, *Faith and Culture* (New York: Oxford University, 1953). Meland says (p. 108) that "Wieman was to sharpen his thinking upon God in a more explicit preoccupation with the future occurrent, identifying his process thinking more exclusively with the modernist motif that took emergence more seriously than persistence. . . . Creativity, in Whitehead's thought, is equivalent, in process thinking, to the Aristotelian term 'matter.' It is the basic on-goingness of bare, brute force. The ordering, creative activity of God, with the aid of ideal forms, constantly presses this aimless Creativity into actualized, meaningful events. Wieman has fused these three concepts into one. Creativity, for him, carries the complex meaning of on-goingness, integration, appreciative awareness of possibilities, and the consequent of all these, deepening community." (Cf. further Wieman's *The Source of Human Good* [University of Chicago Press, 1946], pp. 58 f.)

Meland is critical of Wieman's construction, and attempts further distinctions, particularly to bring past experience more actively into focus as an important factor in creativity. E.g., "the structure of experience in any age is the context of feeling in which past valuations persist by reason of God's creative working. It is, as it were, the reservoir of inherited wisdom, awaiting renewal in cognitive form whenever the impulse toward qualitative attainment shall motivate experience" (p. 111).

personality out of the newborn infant and brings to greatness every life that attains greatness. This power in our midst is the creative source of all human good; this a man must learn to serve above all, and he must undergo whatever transformation it may require.

Our hope and our courage must come from the assurance that this creative power will always produce a better life whenever conditions permit; but the better life will always be a life different from what we now live, with interests finding fulfillment in other ends than those we seek. . . . This is true, no matter how righteous and noble our plan and order of life may seem to be, so long as it is shaped within the limits of our perspective and bias; and it is always so limited. If maintained triumphantly to the end, it would suffocate hope, destroy fulfillment and leave life a barren waste. . . . (Pp. 130–131)

Not the hope that sees the end can give us courage to fight with power, but a faith that lives in the keeping of a creativity able to bring forth a good we cannot see. . . . This is not credulity but understanding. We know that there is a creative might rearing a good we cannot discern at the time: when we look backward after many years, perhaps many generations, we can see the new creations invisibly emerging in the midst of the labors and the breakdown of lives participant in the creation, if these lives were devoted to this creative interchange and provided the conditions needed for it to work effectively. . . . We must be broken because there is a God who works for righteousness so great that it cannot be confined to the limits of our control. We must be broken because there is, day by day, the creation of a kingdom of goodness in depth and height and scope so far beyond the reach of any human plan that it must not be constricted to our imposed directive. (Pp. 132–133)

One can agree with the truth in Wieman's statements about the creative in history, even though one may suspect that the viewpoint involves a very selective reading of the events which sustain the case. And one can appropriate the truth here emphasized without necessarily taking with it the whole framework of process theology.

Still another perspective from which to view the creative is provided by modern archaeology. The theory of evolution as originally expounded in the last century involved the assumption that the movement was always in one direction, toward future emergents and higher ideals. Thus philosophy, education, and theology were dominantly oriented toward future events. In Old Testament study, this meant that the high point and center of concentration lay in Second Isaiah (Chaps. 40–55) and in the New Testament. Earlier literature in the Old Testament was at a more "primitive" level, and while needed for historical understanding it could safely be discarded in constructive thinking. Yet, as a matter of actual fact, archaeology presents as much evidence of evolution in a downward direction as it does of evolution toward increasing complexity in thought and technology. The typical example is the sudden flowering of a new culture which is at its best in its earliest period. Then follow decline and decay, which may suddenly be interrupted by a new flowering of creativity. At the same time, individual artifacts have their individual histories which may or may not be affected by the birth and decline syndrome of major cultural epochs in which they evolve.

In other words, many phenomena are at their finest degree of development when first encountered. They always can be shown to arise in an environment to which they are related; they have vital links with what preceded them—or so it would appear where we have sufficient evidence for study. Nevertheless, they are generally startling new emergents for which the historian's cause and effect chain has no proper explanation. Illustrations are the sudden development of the first known monumental architecture in the temples of Mesopotamia during the Obeid culture of the fourth millennium B.C., or the sudden impulses toward urbanism which characterized Early Bronze I (ca. 3200–2900 B.C.) and Middle Bronze II A (ca. 1900–1750 B.C.) in Palestine. The religio-political system of Mosaism is another such phenomenon, though it must be reconstructed by hypothesis, like most ancient history, from generally later materials.

In other words, a pattern which involves a sudden bursting forth of creativity, then adaptation, perhaps development of individual

features and decline, is clearly to be observed repeatedly in various
periods of human history. If one chooses to do so, one can readily
relate it to Israel's conception of the creative in history. Yet the
sudden emergents cannot be predicted in advance; they can only
be observed and studied in relation to their environments. Nor can
they be projected as the only things occurring; many other happenings with their own individual histories are going on at the same
time. From one point of view, then, history is chaos, and the historian attempts to sort out and relate what he regards as the most
significant and important movements while disregarding what he
considers factors of lesser importance. If there is a creative providence of God in history, it can only be observed in faith. It cannot
be predicted as so regular and dependable that faith and commitment, so often working in the dark, can simply be dispensed with.
Yet faith is more than "whistling in the dark"; it is a commitment
to what appears to be reasonable and to positive goals of action
derived therefrom (see Chap. 2).

   If one can observe evolution toward decay, no matter the complexities and contradictions in the overall picture of a period, he
can certainly observe it proceeding in the opposite direction also,
provided that a large enough perspective is employed. Here too,
however, simplistic viewpoints must be avoided, and the dangers of
generalization are acute.

   The origin of man, though a great concern to Near Eastern man
and to so many primitive religions, did not become a respectable
subject for western science until the archaeological discovery during
the middle of the last century of man-made tools in association with
long extinct forms of life preserved in fossil form, and until Darwin's *On the Origin of Species* in 1859, and, subsequently, his
Descent of Man in 1871. Today we can say that if the first signs
of life appeared at least some three billion years ago, then 98 per
cent of the history of life on earth had passed before primates appeared during the Paleocene period of geology (over sixty million
years ago?). Among the primates, anthropoid apes made their appearance in due course, and these are closest to man in physical
structure. Varieties of these apes are found today only in south-
east Asia and in west and central Africa. Indeed, the earliest homi-

nids appear to have branched off from among the chimpanzees and gorillas which today are only found in Africa. This fact, coupled with the archaeological discoveries in Africa, led Teilhard de Chardin to write in 1952, before the discoveries by Leakey and others since that time, as follows:

> Under the pressure of so much evidence, it becomes both difficult and unscientific not to accept the idea that the Dark Continent (the last to have been opened to scientific investigation) is precisely the one which, during the Upper Cenozoic period, acted as the main laboratory for the zoological development and the earliest establishment of man on this planet.

> It is apparently in the depths of Africa (and not on the shores of the Mediterranean Sea or on the Asiatic plateau), therefore, that the primeval center of human expansion and dispersion must have been located, long before this center shifted, in much later times, toward (or even split between) Eurasia and America.[14]

As it now well-known, L. S. B. Leakey has found at least three varieties of hominids in the geological layers of the Olduvai gorge in Tanzania, east Africa, which date between one and two million years ago. These beings are distinguished by the facts that, among other characteristics, they walked upright on two feet, they possessed fully developed the remarkable human hand, and they used fairly crude types of chipped stone tools. One of the tools was a fairly large fist chopper and the other a tool made by striking a roundish stone in such a way as to form a cutting edge. Dr. Leakey claims that he and his sons have killed a deer and have attempted to skin it with their teeth, but found that they could not do so. Yet with a bit of practice they learned that they could make a cutting

---

[14] From a paper entitled "The Idea of Fossil Man," read before an anthropological conference in New York during June, 1952. It was published along with other papers from the conference in a volume ed. by Sol Tax, *Anthropology Today* (now available in paperback from the University of Chicago Press, Phoenix Books, 1962), pp. 31–38 (quotation from p. 34).

tool of stone in some thirty seconds, which made the skinning a comparatively easy process.[15]

Along the land bridge between Eurasia and Africa, the earliest human artifacts thus far found have been by Stekelis and his associates at Abbeidiyeh, a short distance south of the Sea of Galilee in Israel. The stone tool horizon is precisely that of Dr. Leakey in Kenya, and the date of the associated fossils of extinct forms of life along the shores of the inland lake that once was the whole Jordan Valley has been calculated at about one million years. This discovery was exciting news to Dr. Leakey, because for man to have gotten to Europe and to eastern Asia during the much earlier Miocene-Pliocene era, he would have had to cross the Palestinian land bridge.

Neanderthal man, dating from the middle of the Paleolithic or Old Stone Age (*ca.* 75,000–50,000 years ago) seems to have been a special development largely confined to Europe. While he used chipped stone tools, had a brain cage capacity as large or larger than modern man, and walked upright, he looked more apelike than some of his predecessors. Elsewhere, in the Mt. Carmel caves of Palestine, for example, people very much like ourselves were living at the same time. Today the earth is peopled by one type of this man, Homo sapiens, who seems to have been one of the latest of the species of hominids to develop. While we do not know where or when his type began, most witnesses so far found to his existence begin some 35,000 years ago.[16] Older varieties of man did not sur-

[15] From an address given by Leakey in Jerusalem before the Israeli Academy of Arts and Sciences during the winter of 1964–1965. The earliest fossils which are distinguished as hominids are much earlier than anything thus far found in Olduvai gorge and are perhaps as early as fourteen or more million years ago. For recent discussion with bibliography, see Bernard Campbell, *Human Evolution* (Chicago: Aldine Publishing Co., 1966), pp. 326–366.

[16] Most scientists have thought of Homo sapiens as being post-Neanderthal. Yet the origin of the type appears to go back as early as fossils found in Swanscombe in England and Steinheim in Germany, dating *ca.* 150,000–250,000 years ago. Neanderthal man is perhaps a European pocket which in time was virtually surrounded and then

vive because they were unable to adapt or compete in environments which they could not survive.

It was Homo sapiens who in the Near East some nine thousand years ago ushered in the Neolithic revolution, which established the first villages and some five thousand years later achieved the social organization and technological control of his environment, which enabled him to establish cities, states, and empires. While doing so, he learned and transmitted to us, who are his progeny, things which are basic to our culture about living together in communities, about beauty, grace, and righteousness, about literature and the arts, about history and science. Indeed, modern history and science are solely western developments of this man. They appear to have been made possible by the demything of nature in two different ways of which we are heir. One was by the Greeks, who claimed reality to be rational, and one by the Israelites, who claimed the world of the gods to be the creation of one Suzerain, who established man in his service as king over the earth. The demything of nature set man free to explore it, while it brought time and history to the forefront of western consciousness.

In other words, perhaps the two most important events in earth's evolution have been the emergence of life and the emergence of Homo sapiens. At every stage of life's development some element of transcendence has been present, wherein certain types of living things outstrip and rise above the limits of their environments and of their own chemical and physical processes. As one of our leading zoologists states:

> Adaptive response to environmental challenges is the main-spring of biological evolutionary transcendence in man's origin from his prehuman ancestors. . . . Man is not only a tool user but also a tool maker; he is capable of symbolic and abstract thought; he communicates by means of symbolic language; he has created culture, which is transmitted not by genes but by teaching and learning. By any reasonable criteria,

---

eliminated by vigorous moderns like the comparatively tall Cro-Magnons of the Upper Paleolithic (*ca.* 25,000 years ago) and those responsible for the swift refinement of tools and for the remarkable cave printings in southern France and northern Spain.

man is the most successful biological species in existence. He adapts his environments to his genes more frequently and efficiently than his genes to his environments.[17]

Indeed, man's power of thought and his social organization now enable him to plan his future, to adapt his environment, and to govern his own evolution. Thus, with full confidence, needing only time and money, he is now about to adapt his earthly being to the inhospitable moon.

Here again the evolutionary perspective enables one to see manifold evidence of the creative in earth's history. Yet the evolution has been no simple thing. Forms of life like the dinosaurs and Neanderthalers evolve and then die out. Areas of life stagnate: most American Indians, the Australian aborigines, and many natives of Africa never on their own emerged from the Stone Age. Modern history is full of the conflict of the more adaptively advanced people against those less advanced. Mexico and Peru flowered spectacularly in this hemisphere for a time, but then were quickly extinguished, leaving no influence on modern life. Islamic peoples, and others in central and eastern Asia, have all had their times of glory. Yet present and future appear to belong to those trained in western technology, the ultimate roots of which go back to Rome, Greece, and the ancient Near East. There seems to be no power on earth the equal of this technology. The so-called "Christendom" of the European and American variety is synonymous with the greatest mastery of nature the world has known. This particular creation of Homo sapiens in our time makes western man indeed what the Bible claimed for him, king over the earth. A comparative newcomer in earth's time-span now has power to determine what other forms of life may exist beside him, while he exploits nature with an orgy limited only by his desire, knowledge, and profit.

How is it possible to view this "secular city" of modern man in the perspective of the creative? A basic proposition of Teilhard de Chardin is as follows: In the processes of life from the very begin-

[17] T. Dobzhansky, "Evolution: Implications for Religion," *Christian Century,* July 19, 1967, pp. 936–941.

ning there has been an inner dynamism which has pushed continuously for the emergence of ever more complex forms of life until the climax has been reached in Homo sapiens.[18] A model is seemingly presented in the evolutionary recapitulation through which a human fetus passes in the womb on its compulsive way toward emergence as a human being. As soon as the egg is fertilized in the womb, an inner dynamism is immediately present which will determine the path followed in the development of the fetus, with the baby to be born in nine months already predetermined.

This model, which leads to some variation of orthogenesis as the explanation for the evolutionary process,[19] seems to make most biologists acutely unhappy. In the words of Harvard's Professor Ernst Myer, man is an "incredibly lucky accident," a "most improbable event."[20] The invertebrates did not appear until after 90 per cent of the time life has existed on earth had elapsed. Among the vast array of invertebrates came the primates; from these came the apes, and from only one of these came man. Evolution exhibits so many "fits and starts," so many possibilities explored, that, on any close review, the dominance of what appears to be the "accidental" seems to be required.

A further consideration is the fact that adaptation to a changing environment appears to be the key to unraveling the history of

[18] Pierre Teilhard de Chardin, *The Phenomenon of Man* (New York: Harper Torchbook, 1961), esp. pp. 58–62.

[19] G. G. Simpson, *The Meaning of Evolution* (New Haven and London: Yale University Press, 1949—available in paperback, 13th printing, 1964), p. 132, n. 1, defines this conception as follows: "Evolution in a straight line is commonly called 'orthogenesis.' . . . The term has, however, been kicked around so much that hardly any two students mean exactly the same thing when they use it. To some it means little more than that evolution is not completely random. To others, use of the term implies granting the whole finalist thesis of undeviating progress toward a goal. Arguments over orthogenesis are unduly obscured and complicated by entirely unimportant semantic difficulties. It usually is understood, however, to mean a postulated inner urge or inherent tendency for evolution to continue in a given direction."

[20] Remarks used in a lecture on human evolution in the Amos Fortune Forum, Jaffrey Center, N.H., July 26, 1968.

man's evolution.[21] Whatever became so specialized in one environment that it could not adapt to change, died out. A changing environment and human behavior in relation to it seem to be the all-important clue to meaning. Homo sapiens won out and reached his present peak of power in the west because his adaptation has been the most phenomenally successful part of the whole evolutionary story.

This viewpoint is in close accord with what was said in the last chapter about man as a historical being and about a theological conception of revelation as involved deeply with an understanding of truth revealed within the changing forms of history. An illustration of the point may be provided by the differing conceptions of man which ultimately lie behind current birth control and abortion debates. One is an ontological conception: As soon as the egg is fertilized in the womb, all of the potentialities which form the future person are already present. Abortion, therefore, is the equivalent of homicide. The demands of a law court force an artificial age of the fetus to be set as the point when the protection of law is extended to it. Yet, whether that age-figure is fixed at six weeks or two months, it is a matter of legal casuistry as far as the overall conception is concerned.

The social or historical conception of man argues as follows: True, the potentialities are all there—indeed, such a tremendous number of potentialities that it would be difficult to say in what direction the individual to emerge from the fetus will develop. The basic factors which determine human individuality are not ontologically present in the fetus. They are socially constructed as the individual reacts to and with his particular environment, one provided by his parents, community, culture, education, vocational choices, and a multitude of formative influences in the interaction with one's fellows, known or unknown, friends or enemies. That is, a person is not simply to be known as an individual in isolation. He

[21] This is central to the presentations of Ernst Myer mentioned above and to the excellent review of the evidence in the work of Bernard Campbell cited in n. 15. An explanation of this aspect of man's evolutionary history in the light of the evidence is to be found in G. G. Simpson's *The Meaning of Evolution* (see n. 19), pp. 123–279.

is what he is in all his complex relationships, in the choices he makes or is forced to make by the many opportunities which open ahead of him, etc.

Similarly, an ontological view of the evolutionary process which leads to some form of orthogenesis can scarcely be sustained by what the eye and mind can observe and expound. It is instead life challenged by physical and social opportunities, choosing, taking chances, laying plans, either failing or succeeding by trial and error, but in the end triumphant over the problems and challenges. This is the context in which the signs of human evolution are to be interpreted, just as it is today the context in which personality takes form and successfully adapts itself to its environment, or the environment to itself, or else fails to do either.[22]

The problem of speaking meaningfully about God the Creator from the perspective of human evolution now becomes similar to the problem of speaking about God as Lord of history. One cannot mean that a determinism, like wisdom in Proverbs 8, was coexistent with creation, so that signs of teleology (movement toward a predetermined goal) can easily be observed or described in the happenings of time.[23] One can posit the controlling power of God in history, but the evidence will not permit much determinism. Instead, freedom and opportunities which are seized or neglected, each with appropriate results, must always be kept centrally in focus.[24]

To argue that the creative in history is a phenomenon even more

---

[22] Cf. Chap. 12 in Simpson, *op. cit.*, entitled "The Opportunism of Evolution." By this term he means that "the course of evolution follows opportunity rather than plan. . . . Boundless opportunity for evolution has never existed. . . . Possible ways of life are always restricted in two ways: the environment must offer the opportunity and a group of organisms must have the possibility of seizing this opportunity" (pp. 160–161).

[23] This was the direction of thought within Israel's wisdom movement which led to its rejection in Job and Ecclesiastes.

[24] For further provisos which apply to the concept of God the Creator as well as to the Lord of history, see Gordon D. Kaufman, "On the Meaning of 'Act of God,' " *Harvard Theological Review*, Vol. 61.2 (April, 1968), pp. 175–201.

central to the understanding of the world's life than decay or death, is not an unreasonable argument. It is to be observed within evolutionary processes that are seemingly contradictory, that is, moving in opposite directions. That the creative is a more centrally important element to observe than decay or death can be assumed from the fact that life has gone on, but more than that, it has actually moved into ever greater complexity at an ever-increasing tempo. Decay and death are very real, but life moves on and its creative forces unpredictably surface in unexpected ways, death serving as stimulus rather than as deterrent.

To argue from the creative in history to the Biblical Creator is not unreasonable when the context of Biblical assertions about the Creator and the Redeemer is observed (see above). To be sure, concrete forms of historical redemption which lead to a future confidently hoped for, are only one form of the appearances of the creative. The latter is continually throwing off signs of the Creator's activity, or indeed is the sign of the Creator's activity, for observations of human evolution or of human history cannot be used to identify the Creator with the signs of creative activity. We are here faced with the boundary of the known, and with no more than signs which reasonably seem to point beyond it (see further, Chap. 6).

In conclusion, it may be said that in Wieman's picture of the creative to which reference was made above, there appears what might be regarded as human sentimentality to the effect that conflict is evil and that God is directing the creative toward socially ennobling ends. This may have some validity, and it is good eschatology. Yet, in the history through which we yet must move, the question must be raised whether the unrealistic sentiment behind so much talk about "love" must give way to a more positive concept of conflict.

Two opposing views of our human situation appear to be possible. One is the remarkable story of the accomplishments of the European-American branch of Homo sapiens, the pinnacle of evolution, the unchallenged king of his ever-expanding world—this story suggests that the future is open and wonders will never cease. The other story, equally real, is the radical disillusionment with ourselves, the failure of ideals and the vision of chaos and meaninglessness. This failure of ideals and disillusionment is accentuated by the radical gap between ourselves and the poor of the world. In our own nation, about one person in every five or six could disappear beneath the sea and never be missed. Most of the world has been left behind. Like wealthy people everywhere, we dream of peace and luxury when we are surrounded by the poor. And where there is such great poverty, there can be no peace.

These are the two possible pictures of man: one of his glory and the other of his misery, and both seem to be true at the same time.

One place where the juncture of the two pictures takes place is in a further observation concerning human evolution. At its very center lies not peace but a sword, not rest but conflict, not happiness but turmoil. Homo sapiens is indeed the most adaptable and the most powerful creature of all time. But thus far his adaptations have been accomplished only at the price of continuous conflict, continuous trouble, soul-searching debate within and without, so that he is continually tense and uneasy. In the words of one of Thornton Wilder's plays, we have made it since the Ice Age only *By the Skin of Our Teeth.* Adaptation means change, continuous growth, and determination to peer into the unknown boundaries of existence. The glory and misery appear together in this conflict.

One way to put it is that as human beings we dislike the continuous tension of conflict which adaptation and change require. We thus very easily equate love with maintaining things as they are, with the defense of our fixations. The struggle for survival then becomes a struggle against growth, and evil becomes defined as all sources of conflict which disturb the spot we have reached. The search for safety, contentment, and happiness—life without conflicts within and without—these for so many Christians have become the solid goals of Christian "love." Yet this world of "love" is a dangerous illusion. Where life is fed on the illusion that love and conflict are natural opposites, there one finds stagnation. The evolution of the race, the continued direct confrontation with the needs of growth and adaptation, have their seeds in hope and the promise of what is not yet. To be a full member of the species Homo sapiens requires a life of choices before opportunities. Anything less will consign one to the heap of human beings who belong to the stagnate, the infertile, who have lost capacity for creativity.[25] Life is put together and finds its true freedom only in the struggle for what must be hoped for but not yet born.

IV Summary

When one begins to ask questions about the doctrine of creation, he observes that religions which have it are under an inner compulsion derived from their conceptions of human existence. For Israel creation was inferring that life as known under covenant was fixed in the created order. Creation identifies the Lord of the world, under whom man finds his identity and way of life. In the epic literature, Second Isaiah, and the royal theology in Jerusalem, Israel understood creation in terms of power and purpose. The God who created the world is the same power which redeemed Israel from Egpyt, which will redeem her again in the second Exodus, and which in history carries on the conflict that works salvation for the poor and needy (see further Chap. 5). Creation, then, is not simply the making of the world; it is what identifies history's Lord and releases into time that judging and redeeming power which is to be observed again and again in human history by eyes trained to see and interpret by faith.

If the Creator's work is observable, we should be able to analyze our history and to see evidences of his continuing activity. Those theologians in our time who have made most of the creative in history are "process theologians" who stand in the tradition of the philosopher Alfred North Whitehead, particularly H. N. Wieman and B. E. Meland. Their observations are important and can be appropriated in our search for God the Creator.

Archaeologists know that evolution in an upward direction is only one form of the creative. Even more numerous are observations of the sudden bursting forth of creative energy, followed by decline, which cannot entirely be accounted for by the historian's

---

[25] On the centrality of conflict, and the necessity for it, see, e.g., Immanuel Kant, *On History* (Indianapolis: Bobbs-Merrill's Library of Liberal Arts, 1963), pp. 11 ff. ("On the Idea for a Universal History"), esp. Proposition IV, pp. 15 ff.

chain of cause and effect. Furthermore, the examination of the story of human evolution furnishes concrete illustration of how the creative works in time, and sees the necessity for change and adaptation as sources of continuous conflict in human life. The view of love as passive and without conflict must be changed and brought to bear on this central fact of our human existence.

In some such manner one can today see the importance of the doctrine of God the Creator. The conception cannot be quickly dismissed, for here the Old Testament provides a new and deeper dimension to our common life.

4

God the Lord

I

LUDWIG KÖHLER in his *Old Testament Theology* rightly claims that "the one fundamental statement in the theology of the Old Testament is this: God is the Ruling Lord." "Everything else derives from it. Everything else leans upon it. Everything else can be understood with reference to it. Everything else subordinates itself to it." Religion is "a relationship of wills: the subject of the ruled to the will of the ruler."[1] Hence, Proverbs 1:7 as the motto of the wisdom movement can claim that "the fear of Yahweh is the beginning of knowledge"; that is, the reverence, respect, and obedience which a servant owes his ruling Lord.

From this affirmation the Old Testament receives its structure. Even the cosmos is ordered by it. "Heaven" may indeed refer to the material "firmament" which separates the watery deep from earth and its airspace so that our world appears "like a tent to dwell in" (Isa. 40:22; cf. Gen. 1:6–8). Or it may refer to the airspace above us in which the birds fly (Gen. 1:26; Ps. 8:9 [Heb. 8]). Yet throughout Biblical literature there are the overtones of universal government adhering to the term. Heaven as the abode of God means the seat of world government. Psalm 2:4 refers to the ironic amusement in heaven at the rulers of earth who plot to overthrow this cosmic government. "He who sits in the heavens laughs" refers to him who sits on the throne as the world's ruler. Jacob's dream presents an Israelite's picture of the relation of heaven and earth:

[1] The first German ed. was published by J. C. B. Mohr, Tübingen, in 1935. An English tr. by A. S. Todd from the 3rd ed. (1953) was issued in 1958 by Westminster Press, Philadelphia. The quotation is from p. 30 of the latter.

God enthroned in heaven, sending his angels, his messengers, his officials from the seat of government, down the stairway to earth to carry out the ruler's policies (Gen. 28).

A few years ago, in a meeting of the Theological Discussion Group, we were discussing Biblical images. I remarked that the one indispensable Biblical conception was that of "heaven," not in its spacial sense, but in its sense of a transcendent world government. Let that go, then one must ask whether anything at all can be saved from the Biblical wreckage. Our leading theological ethicist looked at me in amused amazement and disbelief, remarking only: "How far we have come from all that!" The Harvard philosopher Alfred North Whitehead once wrote:

> The brief Galilean vision of humility flickered throughout the ages, uncertainly. In the official formulation of the religion . . . the deeper idolatry, of the fashioning of God in the image of Egyptian, Persian and Roman imperial rulers, was retained. The Church gave unto God the attributes which belonged exclusively to Caesar.[2]

Daniel Day Williams, in a centenary volume commemorating Whitehead's birth, says that

> There is no idea to which Whitehead returns more frequently in his writings than that Christian thought has fastened upon religious thinking a conception of God which had its origin in the despotism of early monarchical social organization. From the earlier Hebrew prophets to the Augustinian synthesis, Whitehead says, the decisive period "begins in barbarism and ends in failure. The failure consisted in the fact that barbaric elements and the defects in intellectual comprehension had not been discarded, but remained as essential elements in the various formulations of Christian theology, orthodox and heretical alike. Also, the later Protestant Reformation was, in this respect, an even more complete failure, in no way improving Catholic theology."[3]

[2] *Process and Reality* (New York: The Macmillan Company, 1929), p. 520.

[3] "Deity, Monarchy, and Metaphysics: Whitehead's Critique of the Theological Tradition," *The Relevance of Whitehead*, ed. by Ivor

One of the main objections of Whitehead to the divine Monarch is that the highest values are achieved by persuasion, whereas the Monarch conception suggests a coercive agency, "brute force," sheer compulsion. Furthermore, moral systems become absolutized because they are issued by a God from a mountain or by a Despot from a throne. Williams, after surveying the components of Whitehead's doctrine of God, concludes that the philosopher "has transformed the unfeeling and unmoved Monarch into 'the fellow-sufferer who understands.' "[4]

We must indeed agree with Whitehead that the Biblical divine Monarch is drawn from oriental conceptions. Is he, therefore, completely unacceptable for modern theology? Does the picture which Whitehead presents of a divine Despot whose chief attributes are "brute force" and coercion agree at all with the Biblical understanding, or is it a crude caricature?

There is certainly no doubt about the fact that the dominant political language of the Bible, drawn from monarchy, has proved so troublesome since the Enlightenment that many thinking persons have queried its appropriateness for our world and have often declined to use it. We live in a democracy which was constructed with difficulty as a reaction to what Americans considered despotic power in Europe. The political literature of America in the period before the Revolutionary War is filled with discussions of power which was thought to be "like a cancer, it eats faster and faster every hour"—"everywhere it is threatening, pushing, and grasping. . . . What gave transcendent importance to the aggressiveness of power was the fact that its natural prey, its necessary victim, was liberty, or law, or justice."[5] In the words of James Madison in 1792, "America has set the example and France has followed it, of charters of power granted by liberty," in place of charters of liberty being granted by power. "This revolution in the practice of the

Leclerk (New York: The Macmillan Company, 1961), pp. 353–372, quoting from p. 354. Williams in turn quotes from Whitehead, *Adventures in Ideas* (New York: The Macmillan Company, 1933), p. 212.
[4] *Loc. cit.,* p. 372.
[5] Bernard Bailyn, *The Ideological Origins of the American Revolution* (Cambridge: Harvard University Press, 1967), pp. 56–57.

world may, with an honest praise, be pronounced the most triumphant epoch of its history and the most consoling presage of its
happiness."[6] Americans fought what we considered tyrannical
power in order to achieve that distribution of power which would
create and maintain liberty and justice. In such an atmosphere, is
it any wonder that the spiritual sons of John Calvin in preparing
the United Presbyterian Confession of 1967 should set aside their
mentor's language and with almost complete consistency avoid all
political metaphors?[7]

II

When I began the teaching of the Old Testament in 1939 at Mc-
Cormick Theological Seminary, I soon became sorely perturbed by
the parade of clerical speakers who said in effect repeatedly: In the
Old Testament we find a God of wrath and justice. We must turn
to the New Testament for the full portrayal of a God who loves and
who is a Father of his people. I was surprised to find the same approach being used by certain progressive Southern Baptist clergy-
men at a conference in Knoxville, Tennessee, in July, 1968. Faced
with the stultifying literalism of the Bible Belt, which lost the Gospel
among the words of Scripture, they felt that the two-god view in the
two testaments left them some freedom to discriminate between one
word and another in Scripture.

Here we have the modern form of Marcionism, which sees different gods in the two testaments. I recall the occasion, when I was
inaugurated a full professor, of quoting to those who cared to listen
the following words of Tertullian against the "good" God of
Marcion: He derided this God as so weak and colorless that it was
no god at all. "What a prevaricator of truth is such a god!" he exclaimed. "What a dissembler with his own decisions. Afraid to con-
demn what he really condemns, afraid to hate what he does not
love, permitting that to be done which he does not allow, choosing
to indicate what he dislikes rather than deeply examine it! This will

[6] Quoted by Bailyn, *ibid.*, p. 55.
[7] See Chap. 1, pp. 24–29.

turn out an imaginary goodness," for the true God "is not otherwise
fully good than as an enemy of evil" and his real goodness is shown
in his hatred of wickedness. He is not God who does not command
a reverent fear and respect, as well as love, on the part of his worshipers. "Where the just is, there also exists the good. In short,
from the very first the Creator was both good and just. And both
his attributes advanced together."[8]

In quoting Tertullian I went on to ask in 1945:

> Why is it that Christians then and now find it so easy to create
> an idol of the God who is the Father of Jesus Christ and to
> set him over against the Old Testament? . . . There seems to
> be a deep reason, one concerned with our whole approach to
> life, truth, and salvation amid the flux and uncertainties of
> experience. . . . My thesis is simply this: We are governed
> today largely by a basic idealism which, regardless of its
> origin, is more akin to that of the Graeco-Roman world than
> it is to the Christian faith. When one looks at the Bible through
> the spectacles of this idealism, he inevitably sees in it a re-
> flection of his own presuppositions; this leads to a perversion
> and coloring of the Gospel. In the Early Church, it was the
> Old Testament which proved the chief bulwark against this
> paganizing tendency. So it must be today.[9]

Because of the situation that then was constantly repeating itself
in clerical proclamations of something felt to be the Gospel, I set
myself to work on the terminological problem of the word "Father"
as applied to God in Biblical times. Here are some of the things I
found out.[10]

[8] From Anti-Marcion, Bk. I, Chaps. 26–27; Bk. II, Chap. 12: *Ante-
Nicene Christian Library*, Vol. VII (ed. by Alexander Roberts and
James Donaldson; Edinburgh: T. & T. Clark, 1868), pp. 52 and 84.

[9] G. Ernest Wright, "The Old Testament—Impediment or Bulwark
of the Christian Faith," *McCormick Seminary Addresses*, No. IV
(Chicago: McCormick Theological Seminary, 1945), p. 3.

[10] "The Terminology of Old Testament Religion and Its Significance," *Journal of Near Eastern Studies*, Vol. I (Oct., 1942), pp. 404–
414. This article needs updating in the light of subsequent research,
but its basic contentions have been powerfully substantiated, never dis-
proved.

1. Names issuing from the Patriarchal, or pre-Mosaic, era of Israel's history fit with those of the Amorite period of western Asia in the first half of the second millennium B.C. These names are not based on the monarchical pattern. Instead, they refer to deity in terms of family or kinship patterns of language, using such familial terms as "father," "brother," and "people" or "kindred."[11] The fatherhood of God definitely has a setting in this culture, and the model of cosmic Monarch seems to play no important role at all.

Thorkild Jacobsen makes a great point of the relationship between this Israelite "God of the Fathers" and the Accadian concept of the personal or family deity, who cared for the concerns of the family and would appear in the family's behalf before the Divine Council.[12] He further asserts, in my judgment correctly, the importance of this concept on later Yahwism, because it gave to Yahwism an intimate, a familial depth between individuals, people, and Deity which other contemporary religions on the whole lacked. Professors Albright and Cross have marshaled the evidence which proves that "the God of the Fathers" was one of the chief deities of the Amorite pantheon.[13] Indeed, Cross's demonstration that it was none other than El, the head of the pantheon himself, clears up a number of problems in Israel's tradition—including Jeroboam I's choosing of Bethel and the El-bull symbol as a more ancient tradition than Jerusalem's Yahwism (1 Kings 12:26–33). Nevertheless, such a patriarchal-type name as Eliab, "My El is Father (to me)," while using fatherhood for the understanding of El, cannot be sentimentalized. Divine family names of this type were used to portray

[11] See W. F. Albright, *From the Stone Age to Christianity* (Baltimore: Johns Hopkins Press, 1940), pp. 185–187. (Also Garden City: Doubleday Anchor Books, 1957, pp. 243–246.) See also more recently, Herbert B. Huffman, *Amorite Personal Names in the Mari Texts* (Baltimore: Johns Hopkins Press, 1965), esp. pp. 154 ff.

[12] For the latter see his description in Frankfort *et al., The Intellectual Adventure of Ancient Man* (Chicago: University of Chicago Press, 1946), pp. 203–207.

[13] Albright, *loc. cit.,* p. 188; Frank M. Cross, Jr., "Yahweh and the God of the Fathers," *Harvard Theological Review,* Vol. LV.4 (Oct., 1962), pp. 225–259.

the close contractual or covenant relationship between deity and the patriarchal family. We are never outside a covenant framework when the fatherhood of God is used.

2. Nevertheless, I learned that during the early first millennium new fatherhood names were avoided because of what Israel considered crassly physical connotations in the conception as used by Canaanites and Arameans. No Israelite, as far as we know, ever knowingly named his child the son or daughter of Yahweh. Such names as Ben-Hadad of Damascus (literally "son of Hadad," the storm-god or personification of executive force in the universe for the Arameans) were anathema to Israel. Yet, beginning with the eighth century and becoming more common as time went on, the fatherhood of God is increasingly stressed in the literature. Contrast Jeremiah's excoriation of people "who say to a tree, 'You are my father,' and to a stone 'You gave me birth' " (Jer. 2:27) with Malachi's consciousness of the terminology question when he says (1:6): "A son honors his father, and a servant his Lord; but, if I am a father, where is my honor, and if I am a Lord, where is my fear [or reverence]?" This shows that whether father or monarch in the ancient world the basic problem was identical. The terminology needs examination in its setting; yet basically the issues are the same.

Another and critical note, however, is struck by the Apostle Paul when in Romans 8:15 he speaks of "the spirit of servitude unto fear," contrasting it with the spirit of adoption into sonship "wherein we call, 'Abba, Father.' " These terms, drawn from liturgical usage, appear of special significance to Paul in depicting the new filial relation we have to God through Christ, which has a formal similarity to the fatherhood conception in Patriarchal times. Yet, considering the New Testament as a whole, the monarchical picture is just as basic both to the teaching of Jesus and to eschatology as it is to the Old Testament's covenant faith. We need only to examine the language of the Lord's Prayer, the implications of the covenant conception behind the Lucan and Pauline versions of the Lord's Supper, as well as the eschatological interpretation of history, for the point to be obvious.

III

George E. Mendenhall's reconstruction of the actual legal background of the Mosaic covenant provides the necessary information for further exposition. It furnishes explanation as to why the monarchical image of God and the language appropriate to it is so deeply rooted in the Bible as a whole, no matter the extent of influence from Patriarchal-Amorite or other familial patterns of language and relationship.[14] Before Mendenhall's work one would usually turn to Johannes Pedersen's *Israel, Its Life and Culture* I–II (1926) for a discussion of the life of covenant as the way of Israel. This great work, now recognized as a kind of psychology of a type of Semitic life, drew its basic model from the world of the modern Bedouin to which some things about early Israel are far more similar than to anything in modern western experience.[15] In the absence of strong centralized authority, tribes kept peace among themselves by treaties or covenants with one another. In this sense, then, it can be said with Pedersen that peace and covenant formed the very atmosphere in which the people of Israel lived and moved and had their being.

Yet, since Israel's basic religious language revolved around the picture of God as sovereign Lord and of people as his servants, Pedersen's model was really not helpful as far as the Mosaic covenant was concerned.[16] His discussion centered in peace among

[14] *Law and Covenant in Israel and the Ancient Near East* (Pittsburgh, 1955, now handled by the Presbyterian Board of Colportage, 215 Oliver Avenue, Pittsburgh, Pa. 15222).

[15] London: Oxford University Press. As has been frequently commented in recent years, the parallel cannot be followed too far because the true Bedouin ideal is a special development within Islam. Around that ideal, however, modern Old Testament scholarship has a similar phenomenon occurring in Israel so that an ideal return to the desert is envisaged. That this hypothesis is false has clearly been demonstrated in Paul W. Riemann's forthcoming monograph, *Desert and Return to Desert in Pre-Exilia Prophets* (a Harvard dissertation, 1964).

[16] A central concern of this particular writer between the writing of the article on terminology (see n. 10) and Mendenhall's first oral

people, a peace whose ultimate sanction was the will of God before whom the people or their representatives vowed to maintain the treaty. The Mosaic covenant presented God as Monarch whose treaty with Israel was to the end that he be their God and they his people. Central words in Israel's vocabulary, therefore, were "to hearken, obey" (*shāma'*) and "to serve" (*'ābad*).

Mendenhall's work is based upon the observation of the close parallelism between the Mosaic covenant and major features of a certain type of international treaty used in Asia during the fifteenth to thirteenth centuries. This was the time of glory for the Hittite empire in Asia Minor, just as it was the golden age of Egyptian expansion. About 1375–1370 B.C., the Hittites suddenly conquered the city-states of northern Syria and the state of Mitanni, a Hurrain (Horite) kingdom existing between the bend of the Euphrates in northern Syria and the region of Assyria along the upper Tigris River. This conquest over, the Hittites found themselves face to face with Egyptian power in Syria. Neither empire wished a trial of arms with the other, and an uneasy truce line existed roughly near the northern border of Lebanon, or more precisely from the region of Arvad on the coast southeastward to Kadesh on the Orontes in Syria, a considerable distance north of Damascus. Following the famous battle of Kadesh in the time of Pharaoh Rameses II, this border was fixed by formal treaty *ca.* 1280–1270 B.C. For Israelite tradition, it defined the northern extent of the "Land of Canaan" which became the northern border of the "Promised Land" in the traditions of the Jerusalem priesthood.[17]

---

presentation of his work at a meeting of the Biblical Colloquium in Nov., 1953. See, e.g., Wright, *The Old Testament Against Its Environment* (Studies in Biblical Theology, No. 2; London: SCM Press, 1950; 9th impression 1968), pp. 54–60.

[17] For Canaan see Gen. 10:15–19 which includes Hamath on the Orontes north of Kadesh. For the "Promised Land" see the priestly specifications in Num. 34:15–17. This revises the text accompanying Pl. VII A of the Wright-Filson *Westminster Historical Atlas to the Bible* (rev. ed. 1956) which was based on an article by K. Elliger ("Die Nordgrenze des Reiches Davids," *Palästinajahrbuch*, Vol. XXXII (1936), pp. 34–73. This article had argued for the traditional northern border to have been determined by the conquests of David.

The Hittites stabilized their borders in southern and western Anatolia and in Syria by a series of vassal treaties, the form of which is unique and confined to this period alone.[18] In these treaties the introduction is always free, unstereotyped narration of the beneficent activity of the monarch toward the vassal. Only then does the monarch list the stipulations which are his primary interests in the treaty. While these are generally specific, related to the particular situation of monarch and vassal, two things among others are always explicit or implicit. The vassal is to have no dealings with other powers because foreign relations are exclusively in the hands of the monarch; and internal peace and order within the vassal's life are expected to be maintained. Then follows the list of benefits or penalties, the "blessings and curses," incident to maintaining or breaking of treaty.

During the years since the publication of Mendenhall's work, so many fresh studies of various aspects of Israel's covenant life have been stimulated that one must say that his thesis has been the single most suggestive and provocative hypothesis of this generation in Old Testament studies.[19] What does it mean theologically?

This is not the place to state the full argument as to why this position can no longer be held. Among the reasons is the fact that David never laid claim to the Phoenician area (approximately that of modern Lebanon), though it is included in Canaan and the Promised Land, while David and Solomon for a time apparently controlled all of southern and central Syria to the Euphrates, including the state of Hamath and other territory north of the Syrian part of the border—a fact which may have played a role in the inclusion of Hamath in Canaan in Gen. 10:18. Provisionally, see the writer's article, "The Provinces of Solomon," *Eretz-Israel*, Vol. 8 (1966), pp. 58–68. Cf. also the brief discussion in Y. Aharoni, *The Land of the Bible* (Philadelphia: Westminster Press, 1967), pp. 65–67, 169–172.

[18] The basic collection of these treaties is in Victor Korosec, *Hithitische Staatsverträge* (Leipzig, 1931). For translation of several of these, see D. J. McCarthy, *Treaty and Covenant* (Rome: Pontifical Biblical Institute, 1963). On pp. 96–106 this author cautiously surveys the differences between the second and first millennia treaties in question.

[19] The bibliography is much too extensive to cite here. See further Mendenhall, "Covenant," *Interpreter's Dictionary of the Bible* (Vol. I, pp. 714–723); W. Eichrodt, "Covenant and Law," *Interpretation*, Vol.

1. The relationship between God and people in the Old Testament was given concrete form early in Israelite life through the adaptation of the form of an international vassal treaty.

2. By means of the treaty (covenant) Israel's self-understanding was that of a people of God in the sense of being governed directly by the emperor of the world. The type of treaty identified God, not as a king among kings for whom the Canaanite term *mélek* was proper, but as "Suzerain," a technical term in political science for a monarch who acknowledged no other power the equal of his own. In his sphere all power was derivative from him. Three implications for Israel's premonarchical religion may be briefly touched upon:

(a) Israel's understanding of power and authority in the world was political, governmental. The Mosaic covenant had government at its center, a government not conceived to be limited by world powers; it was universal in its scope, and Israel, while a special people, formed from slaves of, and outcasts from, world societies, was nevertheless a part of the governed.

(b) The long debate about when Israel became monotheistic should now be virtually ended if the hypothesis is accepted. Israelite "monotheism" was no abstract reduction of the many into one. It was a political derivative, all power being centered in the Suzerain, all other powers in the world gaining their authority from him or else in defiance and rebellion against his rule. The argument over

XX (1966), pp. 302–321; Klaus Baltzer, *Das Bundesformular* (Neunkirchen: Erziehungsverein, 1959, a Heidelberg dissertation which was largely independent of the work of Mendenhall; D. J. McCarthy, *op. cit.;* James Muilenburg, "The Form and Structure of the Covenantal Formulations," *Vetus Testamentum,* Vol. IX (1959), pp. 347–365; G. E. Wright, "The Covenant Lawsuit, a Form Critical Study of Deut. 32," *Israel's Prophetic Heritage* (ed. by B. Anderson and W. Harrelson; New York: Harper & Row, 1962), pp. 26–67; Delbert Hillers, *Treaty Curses and the Old Testament Prophets* (Rome: Pontifical Biblical Institute, 1964); Edward F. Campbell, Jr., "Sovereign God," *McCormick Quarterly,* Vol. XX.3 (Mar., 1967), pp. 173–186. Indeed, the more one studies the subject the less cogent appear the objections of E. Gerstenberger, "Covenant and Commandment," *Journal of Biblical Literature,* Vol. LXXXIV (1965), pp. 38–51.

the meaning of the first commandment ("no other gods before me") should now be settled. An abstract monotheism is not to be gained from it, but rather a political monocracy. An archaic variant of the first commandment quoted in Exodus 34:14 can be taken as the literal meaning of the commandment: "You shall not prostrate yourself before another god"—that is, your dealings are directly with the Suzerain, and independent foreign policies with other powers are rebellion.

(c) The problem of the "kingship" of Yahweh has been very real because of the rarity of the use of "king" (*mélek*) for God before the monarchy. It was generally assumed that Yahweh's kingship was not a part of premonarchical Israelite theology.[20] Now the situation has been clarified and the question is seen in a far larger context. The royalty of the Sovercign Lord of Israel is the antithesis of that of city-state kings. Only with the influx of new Canaanite influence upon Israel's monarchy will a much greater use of *mlk*, noun and verb, appear, yet now with cosmic overtones which allusions to Canaanite mythology suggest.[21]

3. A particularity of the special suzerainty or vassal treaty here being discussed is that, except for the witnesses and the warnings ("blessings and curses") at the end, it is a most unlegal document in the reading. The first part is free storytelling in which the suzerain identifies himself or his dynasty as one which has had a long history of benefactions shown to the vassal, described as gracious activity freely given, unmerited by the vassal. The purpose of the narration was obviously to create a nonlegal atmosphere. Acceptance of obligation on the vassal's part was not viewed as legal necessity so that force would appear as the last word. The context of the whole was the goodness of God. Hence, beyond tragedy lay hope, hope for restoration, for a new heart, for a new heaven and

---

[20] See esp. O. Eissfeldt, "Jahwe als König, *Zeitschrift für die Altestamentliche Wissenschaft,* Vol. XLVI (1928), pp. 81–105; A. Alt, "Gedanken uber das Konigtum Jahwes," *Kleine Schriften,* Vol. I (Munich: C. H. Beck, 1953), pp. 345–357. Martin Buber's *Königtum Gottes* (1st ed. Berlin, 1932; 3rd ed. tr. by Richard Scheiman under the title *Kingdom of God* [New York: Harper & Row, 1967]) was almost a lone voice in opposition.

[21] So Campbell, *op. cit.* (n. 19), pp. 174–175.

a new earth. The interpretation of history, therefore, was drawn from elements celebrated or rehearsed in the regular covenant renewal services based upon the Exodus and Sinai experiences.[22] The grace of the Lord, the certainty and justice of the penalties for covenant violation, and the universal rule of the Suzerain were the main ingredients.

In the light of Mendenhall's work, therefore, it is necessary to assert:

1.   The sense of cosmic government to which Israel was vassal by treaty, a treaty which both gave identity to God as Suzerain and to Israel as "the people of God" with a special obligation calling for service in the world, lies at the very core of any definition of the religion of Israel in the context of the religions of the world.

At this point, an important observation must be made which pre-

---

[22] That is, as affirmed in Chap. 2, and as pointed out by Mendenhall and Baltzer among others, the radical separation in tradition-history of the confession of God's mighty acts from covenant, undertaken by Martin Noth and Gerhard von Rad, is not now sustained by the evidence. Their views envisage the joining of the two traditions during the time when all Israel had come together in the Tribal League and pooled the traditions of the various groups. Out of this situation, they believe, the epic was created. In view of the evidence, only the highlights of which are mentioned here, it may be suggested, as I with others have repeatedly done, that the *historical* results which one tries to draw from the use of literary analysis, whether from critical or tradition history (the latter a much broader term for procedures attempted by the older literary criticism), are simply not to be accepted without question unless one possesses external evidence. See further Wright, "History and the Patriarchs," *Expository Times,* Vol. 71 (1959–1960), pp. 3–7; "Old Testament Scholarship in Prospect," *Journal of Bible and Religion,* Vol. XXVIII (1960), pp. 182–193; "Cult and History," *Interpretation,* Vol. XVI (1962), pp. 3–20; John Bright, *Early Israel in Recent History Writing* (London: SCM Press, 1956). For von Rad's reply to the first item, see his "History and the Patriarchs," *Expository Times,* Vol. 72 (1960–1961), pp. 213–216. Solid historical work, successfully completed, on the Patriarchal period and the relations of the Hebrew traditions to it surely suggest that von Rad's skepticism about the positive value of such research is to be seriously questioned: e.g., the works of Albright and Cross, *loc. cit.* (n. 13), and Roland de Vaux, *Die hebräischen Patriarchen und die modernen Entdeckungen* (Düsseldorf: Patmos-Verlag, 1961).

supposes the discussion in Chapter 6: Not to know how to identify oneself except to say that one is an Israelite, a member of a people created and ruled over by one divine Suzerain, Yahweh, who dethrones the pantheons of this world to subsidiary roles in his cosmic government—this is not to identify God's *being*. While some sort of ontology is implicit, it is not an ontological statement bearing a definition of Divine being. It is instead an interpretation of how God has made himself known in the world and how his actions are to be understood. The knowledge of God is a knowledge of his sovereign claim upon his people and the world,[23] but it does not define or expose God's being which he refuses to exhibit without mystery before the world. This discussion must be postponed, however, for a subsequent chapter (6).

2. The description of the God of Israel and of the God of Christians by Alfred North Whitehead, cited at the beginning of this chapter, rests upon a misunderstanding and even parody of the true situation. The intent in using the suzerainty model is not to present love and self-giving for others—in Whitehead's words, "the brief Galilean vision of humility"—as the highest ideal for human life which has emerged in the evolving process. It is instead an attempt at a radical understanding of Israel's experience of Power which reached into history and made a nation out of slaves, a Power which judges and condemns but in its deepest purpose has defined righteousness as redemption and as loving one's neighbor as oneself. This Monarch is something much more than "brute force" or sheer compulsion or an "unfeeling and unmoved" ruler, who is not the same as "the fellow-sufferer who understands." The purpose of the suzerainty language is to depict why creative, positive, righteous goals have an ultimate support in our world, why life is given for service for which one is accountable, and why, despite the suffering and injustice in the world, life in the service of the Ultimate understood as Suzerain is possible and triumphant.

The opposition of grace and duty, of gospel and law, has played a major role in the history of Christian theology. In the light of cur-

---

[23] See R. Bultmann, *Theologisches Wörterbuch zum Neuen Testament,* Vol. I, pp. 697–698 (English tr. by G. W. Bromiley; Grand Rapids: Eerdmans, 1964; same paging).

rent research, it may be said more firmly than ever before that the Apostle Paul's discussions of Christian freedom and justification by faith over against Judaism in Romans and Galatians are dealing with a specific problem which has overtones that argue against legalism in any form. The specific problem is not one which characterizes the Bible as a whole. The affirmation of freedom against legalism, however, has excellent support from the prophets, from the Synoptic Gospels, and from the ethical admonitions which conclude the Pauline letters. Here the attempt to discover the divine intent behind specific legal formulations is precisely in the context of the apodictic tradition of Israel wherein God addresses his people directly with his "Thou shalts" but leaves them free to decide how a given ethical imperative was to be observed in given situations. This was certainly the case in the original covenant's intention and in the prophetic condemnation of the establishment.

There was a marked tendency, however, for covenant renewal ceremonies to include far more legal elaboration as time went on. The "Book of the Covenant" (Exod. 21–23), the Deuteronomic Code (Deut. 12–28), and the "Holiness Code" (Lev. 17–26) are the chief collections of law in the Old Testament. The first probably comes from the period of the Tribal League before the time of Saul and David, while the other two derive from Israelite and Judean collections during the time of the Divided Monarchy before the fall of Jerusalem. None of them, however, was promulgated as constitutional law; they were liturgical collections for use in covenant-renewal celebrations, as their hortatory endings on the "blessings and curses" for obedience and disobedience make clear.[24] It was the fifth-century promulgation of the whole Pentateuch as constitutional law for the Judaism of the Persian province of Yehud during the covenant renewal of Ezra which constituted the radical departure from earlier custom (Neh. 8–10; see further Chap. 7). This now became the basis for the developments which ultimately were to lead to the Talmud and rabbinic Judaism.

[24] The specific phrase "blessings and curses," from the original suzerainty treaty model, is, of course, only retained in the Deuteronomic tradition. Yet the type of ending in the other codes is the same even where the specific title is not retained.

3.   It is Israel's conception of society under the Mosaic Covenant which is the ultimate ground for current theological discussion of the "secularization" of the Gospel. As vassal of the Suzerain, the whole common life of Israel was the subject of the Ruler's concern. Along with other people in the ancient Near East, there were those who sought to channel the divine imperative through the institutions of monarchy and temple. These in antiquity were the basic ways by which the divine world was related and gave security to human society. Yet the prophetic attack was against this simplification for the sake of the original covenant stipulations. In fact, with Israel's sense of cosmic government to which all life was subject, it is dangerous to introduce the concept of "the religion of Israel." One can either ask, "What is not religious?" or one can say that religion has spread the divine initiative in the covenant to every sphere of private and corporate life. It is by no means the monopoly of an institution.

IV

Yet simply because Israel knew God as Suzerain in a vassal covenant does not answer our modern query: "So what!" Because the Old Testament has it one way does not automatically mean that its languages and metaphors are usable today in an entirely different world. The New Testament must be considered as well as our history and present situation. Without presupposing our subsequent discussion on language and theology (Chap. 6), the following observations must be made:

1.   Religious traditions stemming from the Biblical rootage are the only ones that have affirmed daily work, not as an evil necessity necessarily—though in many cases it may be so because of human evil—but as a vocation for which we are responsible. A tension exists, therefore, between what we are doing and what is expected of us. The heritage of the Biblical tradition is to be seen in the manner in which social and ethical reforms are continually urged upon the majority by a vigorous minority. The American civil rights and antipoverty movements ultimately derive, not from Marxism in

the United States, but from an American "civil religion," the rootage of which is Biblical.[25] Thus, when, on the one hand, we hear
stressed the extraordinary impotence of church and synagogue in
American life, it should be said, on the other hand, that the greatest
influence of the religious institutions is in enlivening the American
"civil religion" and in supplying the "left wing" individuals who
assume leadership in social reform.

The rootage and driving force behind our particular form of
social ideals derive, ultimately, not from the Christomonisms of
piety or theological theory, but from the powerful images related to
the sovereignty of God and the Kingdom of God in their Biblical
setting. Many concerned individuals may consider themselves
humanists in relation to the Biblical tradition and have nothing now
to do with church or synagogue. Yet the tradition is still very much
a living one, giving sustenance to the overriding conception that
dominates the west: namely, that our human effort on earth is
worthwhile, that the worst ills of mankind can be conquered, that
history, while it takes peculiarly twisted turnings, nevertheless is
going somewhere. This is a faith that cannot be proven, but it derives ultimately from confidence that the active Sovereign Lord cannot be defeated.

2. There is a specific type of human relationship which the
suzerainty-vassal treaty takes into itself as model, and which in turn
becomes central in the relation of God and people. This relationship
is a common one, but we have no specific words to verbalize it or
name it. For example, Professor X, a senior member of a certain
faculty, spots a new student, lonely, frightened, uncertain of himself
and possessing any number of emotional problems. The professor
takes the student under his wing, not to impose anything on him,
but simply to offer him friendship, security in a home, and support
as he struggles in his new environment with its vocational hazards.

[25] See Robert N. Bellah, "Civil Religion in America," *Daedalus,*
Winter, 1967, pp. 1–21; and reprinted in *The Religious Situation: 1968,*
ed. by Donald R. Cutler (Boston: Beacon Press, 1968), pp. 331–393;
and John Dixon Elder, "Martin Luther King and American Civil Religion," *Harvard Divinity Bulletin,* New Series, Vol. 1.3 (Spring, 1968),
pp. 17–18.

The professor has given something which the student cannot claim as his right, nor can he repay it as a debt. For the student to do something against the professor in word or deed will probably bring guilt feelings for betrayal of relationship, a much deeper thing than feeling of conscience when certain rules or formal laws are breached. Faithlessness to a gracious person who has given of himself without calculation, giving what could not be expected or earned or repaid—this is a major source of so much of the suppressed guilt in each person. We as individuals generally are recipients of so much of this type gift from other people that one can properly ask, "What would we be apart from what we have been given?" Of course, the relationship can be used in a calculating way as a means of asserting control over others, or one can be completely calculating in his attempt to get all he can from others free of charge.

In the form of a superior freely giving to an inferior what the latter cannot claim as right, we have the human model which so surprisingly furnishes the basis for the suzerainty treaty and for the Mosaic covenant. Its peculiarity is that the gift of self which establishes the close relationship and pulls a response from the recipient can and is put into covenant form, a specific type of legal relationship in which one party takes an oath of loyalty and obedience. Yet this loyalty is hoped to be a personal, loving response, a tribute to the Giver for unmerited favor.

Various terms take on added meaning when considered from this light.[26] W. L. Moran has shown that the verb "to love" is a part of

---

[26] A careful study of the language belonging specifically to the Mosaic covenant as now understood has not been made. One primary term appears to be *hésed* ("stedfast love, mercy, loving-kindness), which Nelson Glueck first showed to be a vital part of covenant language (see now his *Hésed in the Bible* [tr. by Alfred Gottschalk; Cincinnati: Hebrew Union College Press, 1967]). The word appears to name both the gift of the Lord and the response of the receiver of the gift. As such, no English word can properly translate it in every instance. It is hard to improve on the Septuagint's usual rendering with "grace, gracious" and the like. For a discussion of *hishtahaweh*, the common term for worship, see Campbell, *op. cit.,* p. 178. *Nāqām,* "to avenge, vengeance," has long been known from the unpublished work

the suzerainty treaty language. In the treaties, the suzerain "loves" his vassal and the vassal returns his love. For Moran, then, this is the setting for the law of love in Deuteronomy 6:4–6.[27] The term "love," however, belongs properly to the sphere of sex and family. When it is taken from that context and used as a term for special relations of affection in another area altogether, it is not easy to specify exactly what changes occur in its semantic "field." Certainly, changes do occur so that the term is used to describe something familial, close, warm in affection, in the new setting. The "love of God," therefore, cannot be interpreted apart from the Biblical conception of power in action within human society to redeem or to mend the broken, while man's love for God cannot be interpreted except in the context of fidelity to the covenant relationship and a commitment to the social as well as private dimensions of loyalty to covenant.[28] The term "love" is in very common use in liturgy and theology, but there has been too little curb on its sentimentality or inexactness by discussion of its metaphorical quality in a setting far distant from its usual human context.

The point of this discussion, however, is to suggest that the Mosaic covenant is not something completely foreign to current human experience. It is not a past phenomenon in history without relationship to existence now. It takes as model one of the most creative factors

---

of Mendenhall to mean either salvation from enemies or punishment, depending on the relationship of the recipient to the Suzerain (*ibid.*, p. 179).

[27] "The Ancient Near Eastern Background of the Love of God in Deuteronomy," *Catholic Biblical Quarterly,* Vol. XXV (1963), pp. 77–87.

[28] Another term employed in covenant connections is "know" in the sense of recognize one's vassal or acknowledge the suzerain's Lordship (so Herbert B. Huffman, "The Treaty Background of Hebrew *Yāda'*," *Bulletin of the American Schools of Oriental Research,* No. 181 [Feb., 1966], pp. 31–37). The same reservations regarding the semantics of the term need to be suggested, and care used in exegesis of each passage. E.g., the familiar words of Amos 3:2: "Only you have I known out of all the families of the earth. . . ." I think a better case can be made for this verse referring to the election of the Patriarchs rather than to the Mosaic covenant, though in the end the two cannot be separated.

in all human relationships, fits it to the Suzerainty principle in the sense of cosmic government, and thus ties together grace and ethics in what Paul Tillich terms "the ultimate concern." This meets the specifications for theology described at the end of Chapter 2. In attempting to see meaning and coherence in human life it tries to relate what is seen to be basic in our historical existence to an ultimate ground of meaning, however this is to be conceived. And of particular significance is the manner in which this Biblical usage puts love and law, the primary elements of human life, together in the picture of a certain kind of cosmic government.

3.   Yet how do we put the New Testament into this Old Testament discussion? For one thing, covenant is said to play a very minor role there. Hebrews 7–10 expounds Christ as the mediator of Jeremiah's new covenant (Jer. 31:31–34). Paul's tradition interprets the sacrament of the Lord's Supper as the sacrament of the new covenant, with backward look at Exodus 24:8 as well as Jeremiah 31. Perhaps of the same tradition is the Marcan reference to the Supper as the sign of the (new?) covenant (14:24). Yet, John 6:53–58 interprets the Lord's Supper as partaking food of eternal life. Considering the New Testament as a whole, it must be confessed that the Mosaic covenant plays no openly evident role. The reason must be that Judaism's use of the conception made it difficult for early Christians to use covenant language to express the new relationship to God provided through Christ.

Does this mean, then, that the early Church was wrong in selecting the term "covenant" as the key term which held the two Testaments together, and Jeremiah's term "new covenant" as an appropriate name for the body of new literature written by early Christians?

The case for the central and formative role of the Mosaic covenant in the Old Testament has already been made.[29] The case for

---

[29] The history of the Abrahamic (Gen. 15 and 17) and Davidic covenants is another story. The fact that the term "covenant" in the Old Testament refers to more than one type of relationship in no way detracts from the exegetical judgment that the original Mosaic covenant, recreated by hypothesis, was the basic form which furnished iden-

"covenant" playing the pivotal role in the New Testament cannot be made by lexicography or by concordance. The strongest evidence lies in the inner power at work to create a new community which understood itself to stand in a direct relation to the old, appropriating to itself the sacred literature of the old. The Mosaic form of covenant had precisely this central content in the term "covenant": it referred to a new creation, a new community, with a new sense of identity and destiny. This is precisely what the New Testament records. What primarily held the two Testaments together is not only the same God and common understandings of truth, righteousness, and faith, but also the fact that these common understandings held within them this drive toward a new community, the *ekklesia,* the church, not as architecture, but as people of God. Since this is so prominent a characteristic of the movements described in the Bible, it seems quite reasonable to defend the early Church's classification of its new literature as "the new covenant."

4. Finally, if the understanding of God is the same in both Testaments, why is God more vividly monarchical in the Old Testament, while the term "father" for God is most common in the New Testament? In answering this question, one has to inquire as to what the particular content of the term "father" is. This cannot be done by overhasty generalization about the whole New Testament. Illustrations alone can here be given. Nothing is more prominent in the teaching of Jesus than his variety of remarks and parables which deal with the Kingdom of God or the Kingdom of Heaven. Note in this connection the prayer taught his disciples, "Our Father, who art in heaven, hallowed be thy name; thy kingdom come. . . ." That is, the fatherhood of God stands in no tension or contradiction to his kingship. The term "heaven" in this context, therefore, is much more than a place; it is the seat of royal government.

In the Gospel of John, however, "kingdom of God" is a rare

---

tity and self-knowledge to the Israelite, as well as the identity of God. This does not mean that the identity was a static relationship unaffected by past or present experience. It provided a framework, however, in which the sense of national identity and purpose had consciously to be sought out in successive eras.

term (only in 3:3 and 5), while God as Father and Christ as his Son dominates the imagery of the Gospel. In the words of Edward F. Campbell, Jr.:

> But John's is the gospel which explores so thoroughly the theme of the *doxa*, "glory," of God and of his son, a term coming from the royal language of the Old Testament. It is John who speaks regularly of the commandment which the father has laid upon the son. It is John who refers to the judgment which comes into the world with Jesus, a carrying out of God's sovereign rule in the present situation and not in a future eschaton. In a familiar and beautiful passage, John exploits the shepherd imagery, full of reminiscences of Ezekiel 34, to identify Jesus.[30] In short, the presupposition of God's rule as king remains fully in force, and John can be said to have cast Jesus in the role of vicegerent, king because God is king, at point after point in his gospel.[31]

Here again there appears to be no tension whatever between fatherhood and kingship language. It appears possible to say the same about the general usage in current Judaism, which also makes full use of fatherhood terms for deity.[32] Indeed, it must be postulated that the use of familial language was definitely not introduced as a programmatic protest against the suzerainty of God. Instead, the unity behind all the various titles of God in both Old and New Testaments (King, Lord, Judge, Warrior, Shepherd, Father, Redeemer, etc.) lies precisely in the conception of God as Suzerain. The Suzerain as Father and Shepherd refers metaphorically to his familial and pastoral role in relation to his people.

[30] At this point, Campbell refers to Fr. Raymond E. Brown's study in his commentary on *John* (*The Anchor Bible;* New York: Doubleday & Company, 1966, Vol. I, pp. 383–400, esp. p. 383), and gives credit generally to this commentary to sustain his contentions about the picture of God in the Johannine gospel.

[31] Campbell, *op. cit.*, p. 185.

[32] See now Joseph Heinemann, *Prayer in the Period of the Tanna'im and the Amora'im: Its Nature and Its Patterns* (Hebrew with English summary; Jerusalem: Magnes Press of Hebrew University, 1964). This reference was given me by Eric M. Meyers.

If it be objected that Suzerain is not an acceptable model for modern man to use for deity, let it be recalled that "father" for many people in our world has a very faulty referent in their experience. Let it also be remembered that democracy is a system of distributing and balancing of power to secure maximum freedom and justice because no king or other human being can be trusted with absolute power. In other words, any image known on earth which might be used of deity is a broken one. Yet the Bible restores to human terms used for God the fullness of their ideal content, and thus mends what is known only as broken on earth. Whitehead's oriental potentate whose chief attribute is "sheer force" is a myth. Many such potentates lived, but the lives and attributes of none depict the fullness of the royalty of the God of Israel or the Father of Jesus Christ.

V Summary

Israel's Divine Monarch envisages a cosmic government which fulfills man's ancient hope of what government should be. Yet since the Enlightenment many people have found such a model unacceptable for deity. An analysis of the problems involved in the Biblical titles for God, however, and in what is being claimed for the meaning of existence, changes the query into how the Biblical understanding of life can be better expressed. Furthermore, a survey of recent work on the Mosaic covenant shows most popular views about the God of Israel, as opposed to the Father of Jesus Christ, to be caricatures of his real nature. God's covenant with his people rested on a relationship between persons for which the English language has no name. It refers to a superior's gift of self, unmerited, unrepayable, which draws from the recipient a response which includes praise and loyalty. Behind the Mosaic covenant is a suzerainty treaty in Bronze Age Asia which is the one international covenant that rests its case on precisely this specific type of relationship, one which holds grace and duty to be part of each other and inseparable. Forms of sovereignty, expressed in such titles as Lord,

Judge, Warrior, Shepherd, Father, represent the different ways in which Biblical men interpreted their experience of God's power. Forms of power which earthly mortals corrupt are restored their full and special meaning when understood as forms of action experienced in Israel's Lord, who is also the Father of Jesus Christ.

5

God the Warrior

A MOST pervasive Biblical motif is the interpretation of conflict in history as owing to the sin of man, against which the cosmic government and its Suzerain take vigorous action. Since so much of history is concerned with warfare, it therefore must be expected that one major activity of the Suzerain will be the direction of war for both redemptive and judgmental ends. That is, a major function of the Suzerain will be understood to be his work as Warrior.

Yet in our time no attribute of the Biblical God is more consciously and almost universally rejected than this one. The reason is that theologically we are unable to keep up with our emotional attitudes toward war. The latter are so shocked by the savage horror of war that it is most difficult to see any positive good in this type of conflict. As the weapons of war become more efficiently destructive, the harm caused is surely greater than the good brought by success. As a result, the Bible on this subject is simply dismissed, or at best treated in the most simplistic and superficial manner. Jesus and the New Testament portray love and the God of love, while the God of the Old Testament, especially the God of Joshua, is another deity altogether, or at least a lower, more primitive understanding of deity.

Such an attitude is more a derivative from idealism than it is from a faith that struggles with history, with the way men actually act in time and space, and seeks there the evidence of Providence. Idealism predetermines its conception of The Good, and thus ends with a "philosophy" unable to deal with human life as it is actually lived.[1] Hence, the sermons and contemporary prayers in the typical

---

[1] See Chap. 1, and esp. the quotations from Kierkegaard and William

synagogue or church have generally dealt with the inner resources
of faith, though the recent civil rights and poverty problems are
now receiving attention, primarily because the safety of law and
order is threatened. One can see the truth in the statement attributed to Harry Golden to the effect that in his town he as a Jew
can go to church for six months without hearing anything to offend
him.

I

It is the intent of this chapter to suggest that if the conception of
the Divine Warrior cannot be used theologically, then the central
core of the Biblical understanding of reality is dissolved with drastic
consequences for any theology which would maintain a connection
with what most distinguishes and characterizes the Bible in the
world of religious literature.

We begin by recalling a simple and obvious fact about the Book
of Joshua. It cannot be considered to contain a "primitive" theology
of God and war which later books replace with a God of love. The
book in its completed form is an indispensable and climactic part
of Israel's epic of her formation as a nation by the great providential acts of God in western Asia during the second millennium
B.C. Formally, it stands at the beginning of the Deuteronomic history of the ways of God with Israel in the Promised Land (Deut.—
2 Kings). It is a creation of the Deuteronomic historian from old
sources, perhaps during the reign of Josiah at the end of the seventh
century B.C., or else after the fall of Jerusalem, *ca.* 550 B.C.[2] Theo-

---

James about the classical philosophers being unable to live in the
marble palaces which they had created.

[2] Most scholars have concluded that the history was completed at
the end of the seventh century and that 2 Kings 24—25 are a subsequent addition to bring the story up to date *ca.* 550 B.C. A decision
between the two views is difficult. Granted that nearly all the material
used is preexilic, the period when the chief historian drew it together
depends so much on one's understanding of the theological purpose of
the historian.

logically, it furnishes traditional details about how the initial wars of conquest were won by Joshua. Israel was victorious, not because they were marvelous fighters under a brilliant general, but because God went before Israel, threw fear into the hearts of the opposition, and wrought the victory for his own purposes.

In Israel's confessions of faith and praise to God for his marvelous works, the Conquest is closely associated with the Exodus. The slaves who were freed from Egyptian bondage are given a land. The outcasts, the powerless, the slaves of the greatest world power of the day, are now a nation with "a land of milk and honey" as a gift of God (Deut. 26:9). It is the Promised Land, promised by God to Abraham, Isaac, and Jacob (Gen. 12:7; Deut. 6:23). The victories in the Conquest were "not by your sword or by your bow. I gave you a land on which you had not labored" (Josh. 24:12–13).

Biblical references to the conquest generally omit all mention of specific battles and human activity. It is God's deed; he is the sole actor; there are no human heroes.[3] A few citations will suffice:

The prophet Amos, speaking for God, exclaimed:

> It was I who destroyed the Amorite before them
> Whose height was like the height of cedars
> and whose strength was that of oaks.
> I destroyed his fruit above
> and his roots below.
>
> (2:9)

[3] In spite of the number of Biblical theologies which have been written, the task of preparing such a work, in the view of this writer, is very difficult because the basic research work has either not been done or must be redone because of the advance in research. A definitive study of the theology of the conquest theme in Biblical literature is an example; it simply has not been made—or at least not published. It is interesting that whereas Sihon and Og whom Moses conquered in Transjordan are occasionally mentioned (a tradition surviving from the liturgy of celebration once used at Gilgal?), no specifics are ever given in prophecy or psalms of battles west of the Jordan, except on a very rare occasion, Jericho. All activity is Yahweh's.

An early psalm has the following reference to God's work as Warrior:

> He led them in safety and they were not terrified;
>   their enemies, the sea covered over!
> He brought them into his holy boundary,
>   this mountain which his right hand had acquired.[4]
> He expelled nations before them;
>   he assigned them a measured allotment.[5]
>   he made the tribes of Israel to dwell[6] in their tents.
>
> (78:53–55)

Another psalm refers to the Conquest as God's planting of a vine:

> A vine out of Egypt you removed;
>   You expelled nations and planted it.
> You cleared [the ground] for it;
>   its root took root;
>   it filled the land. . . .
> Its shade covered the hills,
>   its branches mighty cedars.
> It sent its branches to the Sea [the Mediterranean],
>   to the River [the Euphrates] its shoots.
>
> (80:8–11 [Heb. 9–12])

Nowhere in the Bible is this interpretation of the Conquest challenged or corrected. Paul is cited as using the old confession in his preaching:

> Men of Israel and you who reverence God, listen: The God of this people Israel chose our Fathers and made the people great in the sojourn in the land of Egypt, and with uplifted arm [great strength] he led them out of it. . . . And having

---

[4] Or "this mountain which his power had created."

[5] This colon is not clear. It could mean that he gave Israel property which had been measured out by lot for the tribes, or that he had destroyed the nations by means of a determined penalty. It can thus be interpreted as going either with the colon before it or the one after it. ("Colon" here is a technical term for one part of a Hebrew poetic line.)

[6] Literally, "to tent."

destroyed seven nations in the land of Canaan, he gave them their land as an inheritance. . . .[7] (Acts 13:16–19)

Stephen in his defense carefully and in detail reviews the same epic story, doing so, however, from the standpoint of Israel's faithless response to God's beneficence.[8] Speaking of the tabernacle in the wilderness, he is recorded as saying: "This our fathers in turn brought in with Joshua [at the time of] the dispossession of the nations whom God thrust out before the presence of our fathers" (Acts 7:45).

More generalized and oblique but nevertheless referring to the interpretation of the Exodus-Conquest events as God's mercy and salvation is such a passage as the following:

Indeed you are an elect race, a royal priesthood, a holy nation, God's own possession,[9] in order that you may proclaim the wondrous deeds of him who called you out of darkness into his marvelous light, [you who] once were no people but now are God's people, [you who] had not received mercy but now have received mercy. (1 Pet. 2:9–10)

In other words, the Conquest as God's gracious gift to those who had been outcast—this is the unanimous account of Biblical authors. In only one place is there a more rationalizing and broad perspective presented from the standpoint of the whole divine purpose in the world. That is Deuteronomy 9:4–7:

Do not say in your heart when the Lord your God drives them [the nations] out before you: "Because of my righteousness the Lord has brought me in to possess this land." It is because

[7] Or "he allotted their land" (i.e., separated their land to their tribes by casting lots).
[8] That is, the confessional history was recited in two ways: one to glorify God for his mighty acts (cf. Ps. 105) and the other to confess Israel's faithless response to God at each juncture (cf. Ps. 106, and Wright, "The Lawsuit of God . . . ," *Israel's Prophetic Heritage* [ed, by Anderson and Harrelson], pp. 26–67). Stephen's defense is a particularly vigorous recital in the second vein. Both are woven together, of course, in the epic.
[9] Literally, "a people for his possession"—clearly an attempt to translate into Greek the special word *sĕgullāh* in Exod. 19:5.

of the evil of these nations that the Lord is dispossessing them before you. Not because of your righteousness nor because of the uprightness of your heart are you entering to possess their land. Instead it is because of the evil of these nations that the Lord your God is dispossessing them before you, and [also] to the end that he confirm the thing which the Lord swore to your fathers, to Abraham, to Isaac and to Jacob. And you [must] acknowledge that the Lord your God is not giving you this good land to possess because of your righteousness. Indeed, you are a stiff-necked people. Remember and do not forget how you provoked the Lord your God in the wilderness. From the day when you came out of the land of Egypt until your coming into this place you have been rebellious against the Lord.

Israel thus is an agent in God's overall purposes as the Suzerain of history. And if one is an agent in conflict, that does not necessarily involve a moral superiority. Indeed, in Israel's conquest it definitely does not involve any connotation of a superior goodness. The evidence is quite to the contrary. Yet as a result of corruption the divine government has decreed the end of Canaanite civilization.[10] At the same time, a new and redemptive purpose for mankind is expressed in the promises to the Fathers (that is, in the Abrahamic covenant; cf. Gen. 12:1–3; 15:12–21; 17:1–8).

In any case, the events in Joshua cannot be attributed to primitivism in Biblical theology. The Bible's most advanced interpretations in later ages saw there nothing but a most dramatic illustration of the power, grace, and justice of God.

II

Now, however, we must go a stage further into something very primitive: the institution of holy war which modern scholarship has

[10] There is indeed evidence of the decline of Canaanite civilization during the thirteenth century B.C. On the other hand, the Israelite conquest in the thirteenth century and the Aramean and Philistine conquests of the twelfth century confined most remaining Canaanites to the coastal regions of Lebanon where in due course the remarkable Phoenician trading empire was developed.

reconstructed from the tradition.[11] In the days before the monarchy in Israel war was waged according to certain conceptions and rules. While religious people throughtout history have believed that their religion and their wars were interrelated, this is something special. As stated before, Israel was a kind of federation of various groups —tribes which in themselves were probably complex in origin— whose treaty together generally, though not always, kept peace between them. This treaty, as we have seen, had government built into it, wherein the Divine Suzerain, who alone could keep the peace ultimately by sanctions against the offending party, was the actual, active, and effective leader in upholding justice, security, and peace.

Every society has its elders whose authority and leadership are recognized. In Israel, the heads of families in the Patriarchal system were the elders who ruled on local problems and infractions of custom. Certain of their number were their representatives in matters concerning the whole League. Legal cases too difficult to be decided locally were brought "before the Lord." That is, there was a kind of supreme court at the central assembly which was evidently held at a place where the Suzerain was honored with sacrifice, offerings, and a ritual in which the great events of Israel's epic were rehearsed for community renewal.[12] In time of national

[11] During the present generation a considerable literature has been written on this topic, following the monograph of G. von Rad, *Der Heilige Krieg im Alten Israel* (*Abhandlungen zur Theologie des Alten und Neuen Testaments,* No. 20; Zürich: Zwingli-Verlag, 1951), also his *Studies in Deuteronomy* (tr. by David Stalker; *Studies in Biblical Theology,* No. 9; London: SCM Press, and Naperville, Ill., 1953). This writer has summarized some of the evidence as found in Deuteronomy (*The Interpreter's Bible,* Vol. 2; Nashville: Abingdon Press, 1963).

[12] For the court, cf., e.g., Deut. 17:8–13; 19:16–19. While these passages are in Deuteronomy, the central part of which did not achieve written form before the eighth or early seventh century B.C., these traditions like so much of the old legal material in the book are pre-monarchical tradition. Appearing "before God" for decision in difficult cases is already specified in the Book of the Covenant (Exod. 21–23), the material in which is generally agreed to be from the Period of the Judges: Exod. 22:9. The meaning of the phrase "before God" is not in doubt; it means appearance at the central sanctuary, as, e.g., in the

crisis, the charismatic leadership which spontaneously arose was interpreted as the Suzerain's raising up his man ("judge," savior) for the occasion. Yet such national leadership was for particular occasions and it could not be passed on to the son of, for example, Moses, Joshua, Gideon, or Samuel.

War in this situation was waged with a people's militia. If the war was a proper one, then Yahweh as Warrior led the battle. The outcome was certain. What was called for was a radical faith and obedience. Numbers meant nothing, and if for any reason a man's morale was not good or he had a divided loyalty, he should go home.[13] In land where Israel was to settle no booty was to be

---

three major festivals each year when all males must "appear before the Lord" (Exod. 23:14–17). For an attempt to reconstruct the meaning of the early rituals, see Hans-Joachim Kraus, *Worship in Israel* (tr. by Geoffrey Buswell; Richmond: John Knox Press, 1966). For an attempt to deny that any such thing as an amphictyony (tribal league) ever existed in Israel, see Harry M. Orlinsky, "The Tribal System of Israel and Related Groups in the Period of the Judges," *Oriens Antiquus,* Vol. I (1962), pp. 11–20; and earlier his *Ancient Israel* (Ithaca: Cornell University Press, 1954), pp. 58–59. Dr. Orlinsky's main concern is that he fails to find any evidence that there was one central sanctuary during the period of the Judges, and much evidence to the contrary. This is true, and apologists for amphictyony have simply held that where the ark was stationed was the central sanctuary for the period it was at that particular place. Albright has argued that Shiloh was the main center until its destruction *ca.* 1050 B.C. (*Archaeology and the Religion of Israel* [Baltimore: Johns Hopkins University, 1942], pp. 103–106). He with others, however, has insisted that Shiloh was by no means the only center during the whole period. The arrangements for peace and covenant among a group which considered themselves twelve tribes calls for some kind of governmental authority. That this was provided by the Suzerain of the cosmic government and his earthly representatives and institutions cannot be denied.

[13] See esp. Deut. 20 for what appears to be an old set of procedures, given, however, in paraenetic fashion rather than in archaic legal forms. For von Rad, *op. cit.* (n. 11), holy war was employed only for defensive purposes during the period of the Judges. That time, however, was one of adaptation; for most scholars the Mosaic era as the creative period and the great period of holy war must be reconstructed by hypothesis as standing behind the adaptive period. Holy war must

taken. No one could enrich himself from the war. Everything was Yahweh's and to be offered up as a holocaust to him.

The ideals of this type of war were preserved for generations. It reappears as the ground for the radical faith which prophets called for, as the setting for the explanation of the Assyrian and Baby-lonian campaigns against Israel and Judah (the imperialists were the agents of the Lord, and the war against Israel was Yahweh's just war), and the Essenes of Qumran possessed a scroll called "The Warfare of the Sons of Light Against the Sons of Darkness." Some of the ideology persists into the wars of the Crusaders. Islam inherited the institution from Judaism and called it the *jehad*. Though the last real *jehad* was the invasion of the nomadic Wahabis during the last century against the western sown lands, one still hears pleas for holy war in the Islamic world to this day. To us the radical faith called forth by the institution is an amazing phenomenon, a type even of fanaticism. Yet without such an in-stitution Israel would surely not have secured her footing in Pales-tine, nor have preserved herself as a national entity in the years be-fore the Davidic professional army was created. Some conservative and literalistic people can find and have found in the vestiges of the institution remaining in the Hebrew tradition support for virtually any violent action or attitude desired.

There is only one theological context in which the institution of holy war in early Israel can be dealt with meaningfully. Certain components are as follows:

1. Ultimate power or "the field of power" is actively experi-enced in history in both positive—i.e., creative and redemptive—and negative—i.e., destructive and judgmental—ways. Yet in the long run I put my faith in the creative and redemptive as the con-text of the whole, because of the manner in which I feel I must interpret the structure of existence.

2. The use of the Divine Monarch theme involves also that of the Divine Warrior because the Monarch's chief concern is uni-versal order. We cannot assume, therefore, that blood and God are

have been the very center of Israel's theology of the era of Moses and Joshua.

contradictory terms, so that where the one is, the other simply cannot be.

3.   Our human world stands in defiance of its pretensions. It is in dreadful disorder, a faithful copy of all the Apostle Paul says in Romans 1 that it becomes when men worship the creature rather than the Creator. All war is fought by sinners who are employing evil structures of power to their own ends.

4.   God works in this world as it is by mediate means. He has his men, whether they know it or not, who serve as his agents, doing what is appropriate for the immediate issue. Our problem is to know and do what we are called to do. But by failure of mind and will, we seldom get our duty straight or do what we know we should.

5.   From this standpoint, Israel's holy war—something that looks to us today as a kind of fanaticism—can be conceived as an agency which God made use of at one time for his own purposes and without in any way sanctifying the participants. Similarly, the world powers of Assyria and Babylon were subsequently used to destroy Israel and Judah—and for just cause, so the literature maintains. Yet each moment is unique. A past pattern of response by an agent can be used as a guide only with great caution in the present. Israel's wars of conquest become no mandate for wars by God's people today.

6.   God the Warrior is the theme that furnishes hope in time. What is, cannot be sanctified for the future because a vast tension exists between the will of the Suzerain and that of his vassals. Our world is under judgment. Wars and rumors of wars are a Biblical reality, a present reality, and we see no immediate surcease of them in the future. Yet the strong, active power given language in the Warrior-Lord means that there is a force in the universe set against the forces of evil and perversity. Life, then, is a battleground, but the Divine Warrior will not be defeated.

Now if one thinks this type of language is too strong, let him only remember that God the Warrior is simply the reverse side of God the Lover or of God the Redeemer. The seeking love of God is only one side of the Suzerain's activity, because, to change the figure, divine love is a two-edged sword. It is power in action in a sinful world, and redemption is disturbing, painful, resisted.

III

We now turn to additional observations on the Divine Warrior from the standpoint of recent Biblical research. One is to observe the way Canaanite mythical language is used to accent the Conquest theme. The first illustration is the manner in which the Conquest is described in the old Passover hymn in Exodus 15:1–18.[14] Verses 16–18 read as follows:[15]

> Thou hast brought down on them
> Terror and dread;
> By thy sovereign might
> They are struck dumb like a stone.

> When thy people passed over, O Lord,
> When thy people passed over, whom thou hast created,
> Thou didst bring them in, thou didst plant them
> In the mount of thy heritage.
> The dais of thy throne
> Thou hast made, O Lord,
> A sanctuary, O Lord,
> Thy hands have established.[16]

> The Lord reigns
> Forever and ever!

[14] For treatment in the light of our knowledge of Canaanite mythology and current Hebrew historical grammar and lexicography, see F. M. Cross and D. N. Freedman, "The Song of Miriam," *Journal of Near Eastern Studies,* Vol. 14 (1955), pp. 237–250; Frank M. Cross, Jr., *Studies in Ancient Yahwistic Poetry* (Baltimore: a Johns Hopkins University dissertation, 1950; privately reprinted), pp. 84–127. For its early use as a Passover hymn, see Cross, "The Divine Warrior in Israel's Early Cult," *Studies and Texts, Vol. III. Biblical Motifs* (ed. by Alexander Altmann; Cambridge: Harvard University Press, 1966), pp. 11–30; and Johs. Pedersen, *Israel, Its Life and Culture* III–IV (London: Oxford University Press, 1940), pp. 728–737.

[15] Tr. that of Cross and Freedman.

[16] Canaanite parallels to this use of early kingship language and to

Here the terror and dread of the enemy before Israel is one of the works of God the Warrior in holy war. Of special interest, however, is the description of the Conquest as God's bringing and planting his people in his mountain where he has erected his throne and sanctuary. This is a reference to the Canaanite cosmic mountain, the abode of the gods, which had a concrete reference point in Mt. Saphon, north of Ugarit in Syria, where Baal had his throne and sanctuary. The mythological language is appropriated so that the Promised Land, the land of Canaan, is claimed to be the cosmic mountain where the gods live and rule.

Another early hymn refers to the crossing of the Jordan (Josh. 3) as God's routing of the dragon Sea, as in the Canaanite creation myth Baal defeats the dragon of chaos. It is Psalm 114 which may be freshly translated as follows:

> When Israel went forth from Egypt,
>   The household of Jacob from a foreign-tongued nation,
> Judah became his holy [place],
>   And Israel his royal dominion.
> The Sea looked and fled;
>   The Jordan turned backwards.
> The mountains danced like rams,
>   Hills like the young of sheep.
> What is the matter, O Sea, that you flee,
>   O Jordan, that you turn backwards,
> O mountains, that you dance like rams,
>   O hills, like the young of sheep?
> Before the Sovereign tremble, O earth,
>   Before the God of Jacob,
> Who transforms the rock into a pool of water,
>   The flint into a spring of water.

A similar use of the Canaanite creation myth occurs in Isaiah 51:9–11, translated in Chapter 2.

---

the use of heritage (inheritance), throne, and sanctuary in parallelism are close and almost precise. Thus, although the passage was later thought to refer to Jerusalem, it need not do so in its original form, since it is almost a quotation from Canaanite poetry.

A major discussion among Old Testament scholars in modern times has been over the meaning of Israel's use of myth in this manner. The myth-and-ritual school has asserted the primacy of myth which was historicized when Israel used it in her worship. The *heilsgeschichte* school, emphasizing the proclamation of the great events of Israel's origin as divine activity, stresses the primacy of Israel's historical sense. Thus, when Israel referred to or quoted myth, she immediately historicized the references and used them metaphorically.[17] Surely, both points of view have merit, depending upon which way one looks at the matter. The problem, however, is this: Granted that Israel's sense of reality transformed all mythical references when used in the new context, *something* of the original meaning must have been retained in the mythical references or else they would not be used. Perhaps it would be safe to say that God's war of conquest likened to his slaughter of the dragon at creation served to heighten the importance of the event. It becomes something of universal significance, far transcending its own time and place. The reference to Palestine as the cosmic mountain where God has his throne and where Israel is planted suggests something possessing more than ordinary significance. Because of the special divine purpose behind the Conquest, the land becomes holy land, the center of the world where the divine government bears rule. And Israel's placement in that land as a special work of the Suzerain is a matter of special and universal importance. While the myth is drawn into Israel's historical tradition, it retains its mythical flavor to the extent that the significance of the history is enhanced and understood as of universal import.

To some degree, anyone who understands the importance which the Judeo-Christian heritage has had for civilization can see some truth in these assertions. Israel's life in Palestine in antiquity has indeed had a universal significance. Using Israel's political language and sense of cosmic government, it is necessary, then, to speak of the Divine Sovereign, who in the role of Warrior against what displeases him and for what he proposes in the history of human

[17] For discussion and references see Frank M. Cross, Jr., "The Divine Warrior . . . ," *loc. cit.*

redemption, is the ultimate power behind the Conquest. Yet, since wars occur only in the context of human sinfulness, one cannot take from such a statement about God any justification for war as seen from the human perspective. That God the Warrior uses our evil to his own purposes is the ultimate source of hope in history.

IV

We have seen, therefore, that the Exodus and Conquest could be described in mythic language. This strongly suggests that the re-enactment of the events was probably central to early Israel's worship. Among the features involved in the worship was the celebration of God's leading his people into the land, a procession with the ark carried by priests, the crossing of the Jordan, and the long journey through the wilderness from the mountains of Sinai. The last mentioned is frequently celebrated in old poetry.[18] An example is Exodus 15:13:[19]

> You faithfully led
>> The people whom you delivered,
> You guided in your might
>> To the holy encampment.

Professor Frank M. Cross, Jr. has suggested that these basic elements, celebrating the activity, not of Israel, but of the Divine Warrior in her behalf, formed the nucleus of the worship at Gilgal. He sees Joshua 3–5 as preserving traditions used in the Passover celebration at that shrine. He writes:[20]

The festival may be reconstituted from the Joshua materials as follows. (1) The people are required to sanctify themselves, as for holy war, or as in the approach to a sanctuary (Joshua 3:5). (2) The Ark of the Covenant, palladium of

---

[18] For discussion and references, see *ibid.,* pp. 24–27.

[19] Tr. that of Cross, *ibid.,* p. 26.

[20] *Ibid.,* p. 27. See also, H.- J. Kraus, "Gilgal, Ein Beitrag zur Kultus-geschichte Israels," *Vetus Testamentum,* Vol. 1 (1951), pp. 181–199; and *Worship in Israel,* pp. 152–165.

battle, is borne in solemn procession, which at the same time
is battle array, to the sanctuary of Gilgal. (3) The Jordan,
playing the role of the Red Sea, parts for the passage of the
Ark and the people of Israel. The repetition of the Exodus is
the transparent symbolism in the processional (Joshua 4:21–
24). At the same time, "from Shittim to Gilgal" (Micah 6:5)
represents the decisive movement of the Conquest, and Gilgal
was the battle camp of the Conquest "when they passed over."
(4) At the desert sanctuary of Gilgal, twelve stones were set
up, memorial to the twelve tribes united in the covenant festival to be Passover-Massot: that is, the festival of the old
spring New Year. It is explicitly named Passover, and the
tradition of eating parched grain and unleavened bread, as
well as the etiological notice of the suspension of manna, lends
confirmation (Joshua 5:10–12). (5) We must note also the
circumcision etiology (Joshua 5:2–8), and finally (6) the
appearance of the (angelic) general of the host of Yahweh
(Joshua 5:13–15).

In these fragments of cultic tradition we recognize the use of
the ritual procession of the Ark as a means of reenactment of
the "history of redemption," of the Exodus-Conquest theme,
preparatory to the covenant festival of the spring New Year.

In Chapter 2 we noted that with the development of the new
royal theology came the theme creation-kingship. While the Divine
Warrior as Giver of the land was still celebrated, the new theology
of monarchy brought new dimensions to the Warrior-theology. The
old fall covenant festival in Jerusalem was replaced by the festival
of the new covenant with the Dynasty of David, an everlasting
covenant which celebrated God's choice of David and his choice of
Zion.[21]

Now the cultus in Jerusalem will celebrate, not only the Divine
Warrior's past deeds of Conquest, but his warfare against the
enemies of David and his dynasty until the whole world acknowl-
edges the Suzerainty of God and of his Anointed or Messiah (see
Ps. 2, for example).

[21] See esp. Kraus, *op. cit.*, pp. 179 ff.; Cross, *ibid.*, pp. 19–30;
Anderson, *Creation versus Chaos,* Chap. 2.

Psalm 24 contains a grouping of themes in a hymn that seems typical of the monarchy. The first two verses assert the creation as the work of God. Then—surely only seemingly unrelated—is a recitation (vss. 3–6) about the identity of the true worshiper in God's temple as "he who has clean hands and a pure heart." He it is who shall gain the Lord's blessing and "victory" ("righteousness" means this in the language of war) from the God who saves him. Following this "Torah liturgy" comes the final lines, probably drawn from a temple liturgy in which God as Warrior returns from battle victorious and assumes his kingship.

> Lift up, O gates, your heads;
>> Lift yourselves up, O ancient doors;
>> And the glorious king will enter in.

> Who is this glorious king?
>> The Lord mighty and valiant,
>> The Lord, the mighty Warrior
>>> [literally, "mighty in battle," or
>>> "Warrior of Battle"].

> Lift up, O gates, your heads,
>> Lift yourselves up, O ancient doors,
>> And the glorious king will enter in.

> Who is this glorious king?
>> The Lord of [heavenly and, therefore,
>> of earthly] armies,
>> He is the glorious king.[22]

We cannot be certain about the details of the royal theology nor of the temple liturgies which celebrated its main features. The reason is that we must reconstruct it from the psalms, which were hymns used in the temple worship, and from prophetic oracles. In none of the material is it possible to separate God the Lord from the active Sovereign who takes effective action against all that op-

---

[22] For treatment, see Cross, *loc. cit.;* the tr. is heavily dependent on his.

poses his rule. That is, God the Warrior is central to the exegesis of psalms and prophets.

Psalm 89 was written at a time when Jerusalem and Judah had suffered at the hands of a foreign army (Assyrian?). Yet at the outset the Psalmist states the ground of confidence in God's power to save because of his covenant with the Davidic dynasty. The Psalmist begins: "Let me sing of thy gracious acts, O Lord, forever,"[23] but the specific acts in mind are specified in vss. 3–4 (Heb. 4–5):

> I have a covenant with my elect [lit. "chosen one"];
> I have sworn [an oath] to David, my servant:
> "I will firmly establish thy seed [thy progeny or descendants] forever;
> I will build up thy throne for generation upon generation."

There follows a paean of praise to God the Creator, who with reference to the Canaanite creation myth "rules the raging of Sea," "crushes Rahab[24] like a corpse; with thy strong arm you scatter your enemies." The personified symbol of the chaotic evil of nature in Canaan, dragon Sea, is here no longer the chaos of nature, but the chaos of history, the enemies against whom the Divine Warrior is victorious. Therefore, the Psalmist can exclaim:

> Righteousness and justice are the foundation of thy throne;
> Grace and truth parade before you.
> Blessed are the people who know the festal shout,[25]
> Those who continuously walk, O Lord, in the light of thy presence.
>
> (vss. 14–15 [Heb. 15–16])

There follows a long passage (vss. 19–37 [Heb. 20–38]) about the Davidic covenant and of the firmness of the divine commitment to David's dynasty. If a royal descendant of David does evil and

---

[23] Or "Let me sing of the gracious acts of the Lord forever." The term interpreted as "gracious acts" is the plural of *hésed* (see above, Chap. 4, n. 26).

[24] One of the names of the chaos monster.

[25] Of victory in battle.

forsakes God's law, he will be punished, but God will not break his commitment or covenant with David. This is the ground of confidence and security. The hymn then concludes with a prayer for God the Warrior to act in fulfillment of his promise, for at that moment of disaster he seems to have renounced the covenant and to have allowed the Davidic king to be shamed at the hand of enemies.

This is a different type of covenant theology than that of the Mosaic covenant. In the latter, the people take vows of obedience. In the former, the Suzerain is envisioned as committing himself by oath (see above Ps. 89:3 [Heb. 4], "I have sworn . . ."). This has the effect of a decree, good for all time. It is, therefore, an "everlasting covenant," whereas the Mosaic covenant can be regularly renewed, and that of the new age will be the "new covenant" (Jer. 31:31).[26] Stability and permanence are the watchwords of the Jerusalem royal theology, and they are based upon faith in the Divine Warrior to subdue enemies. The future, therefore, will be the glorious era of peace:

> They shall not hurt or destroy
>   In all my holy mountain,
> For the earth shall be full of the knowledge of the Lord
>   As water covers the sea.

Nations shall assemble at Jerusalem, accept the law and judgment of the Suzerain. Only then will the weapons of war be beaten into agricultural tools, war will cease,

[26] The divine covenant with Abraham (Gen. 15 and 17) is of the same type as the Davidic covenant. For discussion of the relation of the two, see Ronald Clements, *Abraham and David* (*Studies in Biblical Theology*, Series II, Vol. 5; London: SCM Press; Naperville, Ill.: Alec Allenson Inc., 1967). In a masterful defense of the ways of God with Israel in the Promised Land, the Deuteronomic historian uses the theme of the divine lawsuit against Israel for breach of (Mosaic) covenant. It is not surprising, however, that the Chronicler, writing for the small postexilic community, should center his case in the Davidic covenant. There is a future for the community because God promised it to David. This Messianic hope became eschatological, beginning with Isaiah (cf. Chaps. 9 and 11).

And a man may sit under his vine,
  Or under his figtree, and none shall terrify.
                            (Micah 4:4)[27]

Isaiah 52:7–12 is a beautiful proclamation of God's kingship
and its effects upon his victorious return to Zion:

How beautiful on the mountains
  Are the feet of the herald of good tidings,
He who proclaims peace, who brings tidings of good,
  Who proclaims victory [salvation],
Who says to Zion,
  "Your god reigns [as king]?
Your watchmen lift up [their] voice,
  Together they shout with joy;
For they see, eye to eye,
  When the Lord returns to Zion.
The Lord has bared his holy arm
  In the eyes of all the nations.
All the ends of the earth see
  The victory [salvation] of our God.
Depart, depart, go out thence,
  Touch no unclean thing.

[27] This beautiful passage, quoted in Isa. 2:2–4 and with the extra
verse in Mic. 4:1–4, has usually been thought to be later than either
prophet and editorially inserted in editions of their works. Yet in the
current stage of research there is no reason for not considering it
earlier and purposely quoted in the two prophetic traditions. One hint
of this is the history of the phrase, "none shall terrify." Its earliest
datable occurrence is Isa. 17:2 about the fall of Damascus, presumably
to the Assyrians in 733–732 B.C. The usage here and in subsequent
occurrences are generally references to a future eschatological situation. If the original setting were that just quoted from Micah who in
turn was quoting an older poem, the particularity of the phrase's usage
would have ready explanation. The lifting up of the temple mountain
as the highest point on earth, that is, as the cosmic mountain of divine
abode as in Canaanite mythology, would have a ready setting in the
royal theology which employed so many Canaanitisms. It is to be noted
also that the adaptation of the passage to the prophet's message is done
differently by vs. 5 in each book.

Go out from her midst, cleanse yourselves!
  You who bear the vessels of the Lord;
For you go out not in haste,
  Nor go in flight:
For the Lord goes before you,
  The God of Israel is your rear guard."[28]

The pattern of thought in this passage is a second Exodus and Conquest, which in the prophets appears as early as Hosea 2:14–15 (Heb. 16–17).[29] As the Divine Warrior brought freedom and rest in those first glorious events, so he will do so again to the scattered people. The way through the wilderness and entrance into the Promised Land is celebrated as the pilgrimage way to Zion where in the final days the great feast of all men will occur (cf. Isa. 25:6–8; 55:1–5).

Preceding the era of universal peace will be the Day of the Lord, the day of victory when those "who have walked in darkness see a great light." "For his burdensome yoke, the staff on his shoulder, the rod of his oppressor, you [the Divine Warrior] have broken as on the day of Midian" (Isa. 9:2, 4 [Heb. 1, 3]). The "Day of Midian" refers to the victory of Gideon over the Midianites as related in Judges 7.[30] While the preexilic prophets generally reversed the picture, affirming the Day to be darkness and not light for Israel or Judah (Amos 5:18; Isa. 2:12–17), the postexilic period saw the reemphasis on the Day as the time of victory in holy war and the time when the Divine Warrior in holy procession assumed his throne as Suzerain of the whole earth.

[28] Tr. that of Cross, with only minor alterations: see his "The Divine Warrior . . . ," *loc. cit.* (n. 14), pp. 29–30.

[29] So Cross, *op. cit.,* p. 30, n. 63; see also Bernhard W. Anderson, "Exodus Typology in Second Isaiah," *Israel's Prophetic Heritage* (ed. by Anderson and Harrelson; New York: Harper & Row, 1962), pp. 177–195.

[30] Interpreting the background of the "Day of the Lord" as victory in holy war with G. von Rad, "The Origin of the Concept of the Day of Yahweh," *Journal of Semitic Studies,* Vol. 4 (1959), pp. 97–108. This view is opposed to that of Mowinckel who interprets the Day as the cultic occasion when God's enthronement as king was celebrated in the temple (see *He That Cometh* [tr. by G. W. Anderson; Nashville: Abingdon Press, 1954], pp. 52–95 and p. 145).

In the last days of apocalyptic expectation a central feature was the final battle against the unregenerate forces from the north (Ezek. 38–39; Joel 3:9–16). In that day "the Lord will become king over the whole earth" (Zech. 14:9). For that day the Essene community labored to make themselves ready, having left the evil world for the place where the river of life would transform the Dead Sea, creating a new Eden, according to Ezekiel 47:1–12. Among their literature they possessed a document describing the manner in which this last war was to be conducted between the children of light and the children of darkness, following which would come the creation of the new heavens and the new earth.

The Essenes of Dead Sea Scroll fame are an example of a basic shift in metaphysical and cosmological views which took place in Judaism between the fourth and second centuries B.C. While the Sadducees rejected these views as unscriptural, Pharisees and Essenes had adopted them. They provide a metaphysical background for the continual warfare against evil on earth. There had been a rebellion in the heavenly court itself, led by the heavenly lawyer who served as adversary (Heb. *satan*) in cases brought before the celestial court. This rebellion had been crushed and Satan and his hosts were exiled from heaven in the netherworld or hell. While the initial great battle had been won, so that the Suzerain remained the responsible cosmic power, affairs on earth were interpreted as continuing skirmishes between the forces of Satan and those of the Divine Suzerain. The polarization of good and evil is now given cosmic dimensions and even geographical location. Man on earth exists between heaven and hell, and man's earthly conflicts are a sign of the cosmic warfare. In the apocalyptic sections of late prophecy mentioned above, the final conflict on the Day of the Lord is with historical powers even though mysterious ones from the far reaches of the world. This is now lifted to the arena of cosmology. The war between God and his historical enemies on earth, which must precede God's creation of the new Jerusalem and of the new heavens and the new earth, can now be understood as actually the final destruction of Satan and his armies.

This is the metaphysical backdrop of the whole New Testament, though for early Christians the eschaton was a step nearer than for

Jews. The Messiah or Son of Man had actually come and is a fore-taste of the Kingdom. A beachhead against the power of Satan had been won, and the final day of victory will soon be at hand.[31]

In the Synoptic Gospels there are many references to this meta-physical background of the advent of Jesus Christ. Two illustra-tions alone need be given. In the wilderness temptation Satan offers Christ kingship or vicegerency over all the kingdoms of earth in exchange for an acknowledgment of his suzerainty (Matt. 4:11; Mark 1:12–13; Luke 4:1–3). The other is the vision of the future and the return of the Son of Man "on the clouds of heaven with power and glory" (Matt. 24–25, Mark 13:1–13; Luke 21:1–33). The setting is Christ's teaching to his disciples that they be prepared for a future of tumult, persecution, and false Messiahs before the final convulsion in both nature and history. Matthew especially stresses the point that no one knows the day and the hour of the end, except the Father alone; the disciples, therefore, must be alert, watchful, ready for the signs of the end (24:36–51, 25:1–13; cf. Mark 13:32–37; Luke 21:36). Meanwhile, there will be "wars and rumors of wars. . . . For nation will rise against nation and kingdom against kingdom, and there will be famines and earth-quakes . . . : all this is only the beginning of the sufferings" (Matt. 24:6–8; Mark 13:7–8; Luke 21:10–11). In Matthew after the coming of the Son of Man, he is pictured on his throne in the last judgment, dividing the sheep from the goats (25:31–46). In Mark terrible disorders more serious than any in history since the creation will occur and be followed by the disorder in nature, sun and moon being darkened and stars falling from heaven. Then the Son of Man will come, send out his angels and gather the elect in the second Exodus and by implication a new entrance to their inheritance (13:19–27). In Luke, preceding the coming of the Son of Man, Jerusalem will be surrounded by armies, many will fall by the sword or be led away, captive, and Jerusalem trodden by Gentiles until their time is fulfilled.

[31] See Krister Stendahl, *The Scrolls and the New Testament* (New York: Harper & Row, 1957), pp. 5–17; and Frank M. Cross, Jr., *The Ancient Library of Qumran* (rev. ed.; New York: Doubleday Anchor Book, 1961), pp. 240–243.

All of this material is drawn from a Christian version of common Jewish apocalyptic material. The main point to be stressed is simply that Jesus' teaching about the Kingdom has this as its setting. The Christian community should exhibit in its own conduct the ethics of the Kingdom, especially love for one another and bearing its burdens as Christ had borne his cross. Yet all around were the signs of the conflict of God and Satan. This presented a very realistic picture of conflict in history. The resolution will be at hand, when God and his Messiah conduct the final war as the prelude to the new creation.

In the Pauline writings, as is well known, the same theme is represented in the warfare against the principalities and powers of darkness, against the minions of Satan. Here, too, the symbolism is most powerful and effective, for these powers of darkness have their concrete expression in the structures of our world which enslave us. From them we are promised a setting free, a victory which is our redemption.

It is the Johannine writings which exhibit the most "realized eschatology" of the New Testament, and the least traces of apocalyptic warfare. As indicated in the last chapter, however, Father and Son in the Gospel of John are definitely related to earth in a pattern of Suzerain and Vicegerent. Furthermore, when there is occasion for a historical perspective to be given, the conception of historical conflict between light and darkness, truth and falsehood, is surely set squarely within the setting of cosmic warfare. There is even a rare allusion to this in Christianized apocalyptic terms in John 12:31: "Now is the judgment [*krísis*] of this world; now the Ruler of this world shall be cast out"—referring to the destruction of Satan.

It is in Revelation, however, that the substratum of Christian apocalyptic emerges in full flower, with full use of the great themes, including those borrowed and adapted from Canaanite mythology. While the luxuriance of pictures in the book must represent a special tradition elaborated by a particular Christian group, the main things to observe are the worship accorded to the enthroned Suzerain and to the Lamb who was slain, the various disasters in the cosmos which resemble the curses for treaty violation in the

Mosiac tradition, Satan pictured as the great dragon of Canaanite mythology, the destruction of Babylon, the city of the kings and merchants of earth, the battle array of the Warrior and the armies of heaven against the beast and the armies of the kings of the earth, the dragon thrown into the pit, and the vision of the new age.

> Then I saw a new heaven and a new earth,
> for the first heaven and the first earth
> were gone, and the sea no longer exists.
>   (Rev. 21:1)

The sea, ancient symbol of chaos and evil, is not part of the new cosmos. The new Jerusalem is seen descending from heaven, and the voice of God from his throne announces: "Behold, the tent of God is with men. He will tent with them, and they shall be his people and God himself will be their God" (21:3).[32] This is an allusion to the old Jerusalem priesthood's view of the covenant people as one in the midst of whom God "tabernacles" (or literally "tents"), a technical language developed to express God's immanent presence with his people, though his proper dwelling or temple is in heaven (cf. Exod. 29:42–46).[33] In the new Jerusalem, the very presence of "the Lord God Almighty [the Divine Warrior] and the Lamb" replace the old temple, and their glory so lights the city that neither sun nor moon are longer needed. By this light "the nations shall walk, and the kings of the earth shall carry their wealth into it, and its gates shall never be closed by day—for there will be no night there" (21:24–25).

Thus the New Testament closes with a political picture of the new reality toward which life is moving. The "new Jerusalem," the center of the world's life, is also the center of the world's peace, because the thrones of God and his Christ are in its midst, while all rebellion and evil have been removed from creation—for "the sea is no more"!

[32] The verse seems to be quoting indirectly Ezek. 37:27, and hence requires some such reading as this, instead of the received text's "God himself will be with them."

[33] See Frank M. Cross, Jr., "The Priestly Tabernacle," *Biblical Archaeologist Reader* (ed. by D. N. Freedman and G. E. Wright; New York: Doubleday Anchor Book, 1961), pp. 201–228.

V

The purpose of this sampling of Biblical material is not to make a bibliolatrous point. That is, just because these things are Biblical, one should not automatically assume they must be central to our own theology. Indeed, with regard to the themes surveyed in this and in the preceding two chapters it would be simple to suggest that we forget that they exist. Yet when one reviews the attempts at theology in recent years which proceed on this very suggestion, I for one find much that is not satisfying. The conscious rejection of political language as appropriate to an interpretation of my existence leaves me without a firm anchor to what appears to be my central problem as a human being. That is, how I can see my life as possessing freedom for positive ends that encompass more than myself? Since as a social and historical being I was not a person as a fetus in the womb, but only became a person in interaction within my environment of other people and institutions within a context of relatedness to fellow men with our vocational choices, and within a social organism which has its history and traditions, what is the "ground" of my life? To disregard the political is to disregard this central and social aspect of myself as a self-in-relation. To reduce the language patterns to the family and love with the family, to say that my only need is to be a "brother" to my neighbor, is simply to neglect the larger contexts of my relatedness, of institutions, of other people and nations whom I do not know. Does "love" here become a passion for justice[34] which soon goes far beyond what any model drawn from the family can provide?

Shall I disregard the real structure and history of the self and assume with current existentialisms that my only duty is to myself, to courage, and to "authentic" existence, whatever I may decide that to be? But self-preoccupation is the first and basic disease of the neurotic. It is only as I give my loyalty to concerns larger than

[34] See Reinhold Niebuhr, *Nature and Destiny of Man,* Vol. II (New York: Charles Scribner's Sons, 1943), pp. 244 ff.

myself that I can find freedom from the tyranny of self-pre-occupation.[35]

Perhaps we should say that the first and most important thing to admit about ourselves is that we are simply an integral part of nature and of nature's process. If so, then perhaps ancient poly-theism has its point and the process and power of life in all its forms should provide the chief categories for self-understanding. There is great merit in some sort of process philosophy as a back-ground for current theology. Yet the difficulty always encountered is that set forth as basic presupposition by Reinhold Niebuhr in the first chapter of his *Nature and Destiny of Man.* The first thing to be said about man is that he is a child of nature. Yet one cannot stop there without making the equally important observation that man is a child of God. By the latter one refers first of all to man's power of self-transcendence and to all that distinguishes him in and from nature. Man is the creator of cultural tradition. As phenomenon he creates and lives in a present which contains its past, but he also transcends the present by foresight, planning, even controlling to some degree his own evolution. That is, historical man is equally significant with natural man, and both aspects of our being must provide the terms of basic reference. Nature's process is insufficient to expound human life and history.

Perhaps the easiest course to follow is the popular one today among Christians. That is simply to drop all talk of God and live as a Christian humanist, Christ forming a model of what the good for us can be. Yet here again the structures of historical existence are so complex that the very simple, idealized model thus created from the life of Jesus, one abstracted almost completely from its own environment, furnishes a very limited and limiting context in which I must attempt to face the human struggle with and for civilization.

[35] See above the final section of Chap. 1 for additional discussion, esp. for the query as to whether the popular form of existentialism being used currently in theology is not just as artificial a construction, as an attempt to describe my existence, as any of the past systems, Hegelianism, e.g., that it supersedes. The attempts of several modern

It will be suggested in the next chapter that human beings live with their fellows in a cultural environment in which communication is by a language that has a variety of symbolic expressions to convey meaning. The images or symbols are abstractions of experienced realities by which and within which thinking and action take place. To demythologize is to destroy an organism of meaning because it generally turns out to be desymbolization instead of resymbolization. Without the latter, no thought or action is really possible. And one thing seems certain about my existence: I cannot express a sufficiently comprehensive or coherent set of meanings and values for myself, my fellow men, or my world without the use of social and political language models. Such language is simply basic to my life as a fellow man and as a member of a social organization, which includes but is ultimately much larger and more complex than the family alone or nature alone can possibly provide.

VI Summary

The heuristic value of the Bible's version of the cosmic government has been suggested in this and in the preceding chapters. The particular conception and language pertaining to it are by no means simple, and they are so frequently misunderstood and misrepresented simplistically. However, they successfully hold together the relativity of so much of our human activities and valuations. At the same time they present a structural model which preserves the positive importance of values themselves and their relation to what can be conceived as stable and permanent in the cosmos. In this context all human activity exists in tension with ultimate goals, and thus

---

"sons" of Bultmann to suggest that if existential categories are drawn from "the later Heidegger," the problems of the school with regard to history would be removed, have been wordy but not very impressive: see, e.g., James M. Robinson and John B. Cobb, eds., *The Later Heidegger and Theology* (*New Frontiers in Theology*, Vol. I; New York: Harper & Row, 1963); and the critique of Hans Jonas, "Tenth Essay. Heidegger and Theology," *The Phenomenon of Life* (New York: Harper & Row, 1966), pp. 235–261.

forbids all claims of absolutism for our earthly existence. It sets forth a very realistic picture of the world and its history, holding the positive and the negative together in tension but setting forth grace, love, and justice—positive goals—as the primary context of all action. It presents a much more "secular" and realistic Christ than the simplistic improvisations to which we are prone.

One thing clear, however, is that one cannot adopt the cosmic government model for self-understanding and for communication without a creative attempt to deal with the fundamental and necessary engagement of all life in conflict for continuous adaptation to a changing environment. This conflict too often spills over into overt and often evil uses of force because of our sin and finitude. Hence, if God is Lord, he must also be Warrior. Unless he is, there is no ground for hope, for there is knowledge that human evil is not the last word, that the cards are stacked in behalf of the Kingdom of God, rather than the Kingdom of Satan.

In conclusion, I would like to summarize a conversation with a theologian about the substance of this chapter. This man is one to whom I have looked for guidance as a theological mentor since our thinking runs in parallel paths on most issues. Let me refer to him as "Mr. X." He was reared within a community of one of the historical "peace churches," a relationship which he still retains. I, on the other hand, was reared in a Presbyterian environment which has generally been more a part of the establishment in this country than its critic. Consequently, my basic question about the use of force immediately concerns its proper use, the restraints that must be employed, and some kind of casuistic analysis as to the relative weight of the positive and negative goals of the use of force in a given situation. Mr. X will indulge in much of the same kinds of consideration but in a context in which nonviolence is accepted as an absolute guide to action in conflict situations.

He also agrees with my basic thesis that God the Suzerain of cosmic government is the primary area in which the unifying threads are to be discovered in the vast variety of literature in both Testaments. He agrees that early Israel's institution of holy war was an agency which the Suzerain could be said to have used as a device for implanting Israel in Palestine, without conferring moral value on the agent or the institution. He agrees that God as King, Judge, Warrior, Father, and Shepherd is accorded these roles, not as contradictory expressions, but as deriving from royal language which thus expresses the various activities of the Divine Monarch. He also agrees that the common attitude about that Monarch, as given expression in the quotation from Whitehead in Chapter 2, is a misunderstanding and inadequate presentation of what the Bible means.

Yet when we come to the New Testament, Mr. X says that Christ is the supreme and final revelation of the will of God for Christians. This means that nonviolence and love are always the ethical imperatives, and in situations of conflict they must always be employed in every situation. The reason we must retain the image of God the Lord and Suzerain is that only the ruling power of God actively at work in history can assure the ultimate success of the nonviolent imperative.

Yet since conflict itself must be viewed as both opportunity for change, growth, and broadening, on the one hand, and judgment for failure, on the other, why is it not true that the response of "love" is also two-edged? Love in situations of conflict obviously does not involve surrendering individual integrity, while concern for the needy and for justice to the oppressed may involve the active use of power in ways that cannot be described in every instance as non-violent. Can it not be said that when the absolutes of the Kingdom-ethic are translated into absolutes for the present age, trouble always ensues? In the life we lead we are always involved in mental casuistry because two or more absolutes are in conflict in so many situations we have to face. Nonviolence can always be defended in a given instance as the best means to obtain a necessary and quite specific objective. Yet to absolutize it as the only form of action love can take in conflict would from my perspective and tradition be far too limiting for the flexibilities needed to reach necessary goals when we are faced with the principalities and powers of darkness.[36] In any event, such a position enables me to see far more

[36] Needless to say, I am stating this in the most general of terms, and, if this means a position in general support of a given war, it would not lead me to a self-righteous support of a given "just war" theory as

symbolic value in the New Testament's apocalyptic material than Mr. X has been able to appropriate. For him God the Warrior was necessary and proper in its time and setting, but it no longer can have positive use as an appropriate symbol in Christian ethics.

---

background for that war. Since all wars exemplify human evil in its most virulent expression, one can only set up guidelines as limits of coercive action, such as the Geneva conventions, etc.

6

Language, Symbol, and Faith

How is the Biblical language about God to be received and believed in our day? Israel and the early Christians surely were able to believe in the fact of the cosmic government with a greater degree of literalness than is possible for us—or indeed for almost any intellectual in the western world since Biblical times. How can we set our faith upon the Divine Lord, if he is not that at all!

The basic problem here is the nature of religious language. Beyond that are much more difficult questions about the nature of human cognition, how we think, the relations of words, thought, and action. Here we know so little, and answers, even though partial, require several types of interdisciplinary study and cooperation. The result is that the present chapter must be brief and merely suggestive from one person's standpoint. It cannot be more than that because of the limitations of the author.

I

The economist Kenneth E. Boulding in his book, *The Image: Knowledge in Life and Society*,[1] argues for an organic theory of knowledge possessed by an organism, whether individual or corporate. The growth of knowledge is the growth of an organic structure which is always receiving information or messages. He calls this knowledge-organism in each individual "the image." "The meaning of a message is the change which it produces in the image"

[1] Ann Arbor: The University of Michigan Press, 1956; an Ann Arbor Paperback, 1961. The book was written after the author had spent a year (1954–1955) at the Center for Advanced Study in the Behavioral Sciences at Stanford, Calif.

(p. 7). If it merely adds more information, as for example about Henry VIII, no change in the image may occur. At the opposite pole is a revolutionary change like conversion which brings about a radical reorientation or reformulation of a man's image of himself and of his world. The structure of the image is composed of both images of fact and images of value. "The value scales of any individual or organization are perhaps the most important single element determining the effect of the messages it receives on its image of the world" (p. 12). Anything hostile to the image will encounter resistance. Messages which are favorable to it, or at most require only minor modifications, are easily received. The image is not a simple reservoir of data, but "is rather an organization which grows through an active internal organizing principle much as the gene is a principle or entity organizing the growth of bodily structures" (p. 18). In the growth of images there are models at work, acting as inward teachers, imposing their own form and "will" on the less formed material gathered around them.

> Even at the level of simple or supposedly simple sense perception we are increasingly discovering that the message which comes through the senses is itself mediated through a value system. We do not perceive our sense data raw; they are mediated through a highly learned process of interpretation and acceptance. When an object apparently increases in size on the retina of the eye, we interpret this not as an increase in size but as movement. Indeed, we only get along in the world because we consistently and persistently disbelieve the plain evidence of our senses. . . . What this means is that for any individual organism or organization, there are no such things as "facts." There are only messages filtered through a changeable value system. (Pp. 13–14)

The author does not mean by this that our image of the world is purely private or that all knowledge is simply subjective. One can be committed to methods of accurate observation and to the criticism of others in shared or public knowledge. Yet if a group of people possess, with minor variations, roughly identical images of the world, then the individuals in the group must possess approximately similar value systems.

Furthermore, our images of the world, whether of fact or of value, are built up almost entirely of symbolic messages, most of them received from some kind of teacher. Few of us have been to Australia, but we have an image of it. Transcriptions of messages from nature and messages we have about other people and our relationships with them can be understood as separate "facts," but they are no less affected by the largely symbolic structures of interpretation within us.

What this viewpoint suggests for our problem of understanding ourselves and our world is, first of all, that it is difficult if not completely impossible for us to encounter reality around us without its meaning being interpreted to us through the organism of the self, what Professor Boulding calls "the image." Also, there is an inevitable relativity in our knowledge, precisely because it is composed of relative and finite interpretative models. Finally, our communication of "knowledge" is usually by indirection, through symbols which are allusive and descriptive, rather than precise definitions, connotative rather than denotative. Yet, in any case, it is the image which is the source of action.

II

If these generalizations have validity for human knowing in general, how much more are they true of religious knowledge!

The Apostle Paul in 1 Corinthians 2:11–12 contrasts the wisdom of the world and the wisdom of God in the gospel as revealed to us through the Spirit. He says that "we impart this in words not taught by human wisdom but taught by the Spirit, interpreting spiritual truths in spiritual language." Paul was being criticized at Corinth because his ideas and language did not meet the standards of religious discussion in the Greek world. He was challenged to use the sophisticated arts of philosophy and rhetoric which delighted intellectuals of the time. Paul goes as far as he can. He speaks more abstractly and intellectually than any other Biblical writer, but there is a line beyond which he cannot go. He is constrained by the whole Biblical story and its mode of communicating truth.[2]

Thomas Aquinas asked: "Whether Holy Scripture should use metaphors?" He says that people object to this because divine truths should not and cannot be put forward by likening them to things of the flesh. But, he continued, "I answer that . . . it is natural to man to attain to intellectual truths through sensible objects, because all our knowledge originates from sensible objects. Hence, in Holy Writ spiritual truths are fittingly taught under the likeness of material things. . . . Then is it clear that these things *are not literal descriptions* of Divine truths . . . because this is more befitting the knowledge of God that we have in this life. For what He is not is clearer to us than what He is."[3]

One of John Calvin's central emphases is that all our knowledge of God is by accommodation. "God cannot be comprehended by us except as far as He accommodates Himself to our standard." "What is God? Men who pose this question are merely toying with idle speculations. It is far better for us to inquire, 'What is His nature?' and to know what is consistent with His nature"—or literally, "not what He is in Himself but of what sort He is toward us."[4]

The essence of God, in other words, is inaccessible to us. The chief error of the schoolmen and philosophers, according to Calvin, is that they believed they could discuss God's being apart from his revealed will. Calvin here is giving a faithful exposition of the prophets, and particularly of the text in Isaiah 40:18 (cf. vs. 25): "To whom then will you liken God? Or to what likeness will you compare him?" The gods of the world are idols while the heavenly hosts, the sun, moon, planets, and stars, are all created and named

[2] I am indebted to Amos N. Wilder for this point.

[3] *Summa Theologica*, Part I, question 1, 9. Quoted by Erich Frank, *Philosophical Understanding and Religious Truth* (Oxford: Oxford University Press, 1945), pp. 101–102, n. 2.

[4] For discussion see Edward A. Dowey, *The Knowledge of God in Calvin's Theology* (New York: Columbia University Press, 1952), pp. 3–40. The first quotation in this paragraph is from Calvin's *Commentary on Ezekiel* 9:3, 4. The second is from Calvin's *Institutes of the Christian Religion*, Bk. I.ii.2.

by the Creator. And because of his strength and power not one of them is missing and all are maintained in order. Nothing in creation is or resembles the Creator. Nations before him can be compared only to dust particles on scales (for weighing). Yet have you not heard the news from of old? It is solely this Creator, the everlasting God, who gives power to the faint and renews strength to all who wait for him, to all who put their trust in him. The mystery of God cannot be penetrated by us. No materializations of him can be made. We do not know, nor can we know, the stuff, the being, the essence of God so that we can define him. We only know how he has chosen to relate himself to us. Thus, Calvin's conception of God's condescension, the gracious accommodation of the infinite to the finite, is excellent exposition of Second Isaiah, and by implication of the Old Testament as a whole.

Calvin says:

> The most perfect way of seeking God . . . is not for us to attempt with bold curiosity to penetrate to the investigation of His essence, which we ought more to adore than meticulously to seek out, but for us to contemplate Him in His works whereby He renders Himself near and familiar to us, and in some manner communicates Himself. . . . It is also fitting, therefore, for us to pursue this particular search for God, which may so hold our mental powers suspended in wonderment as at the same time to stir us deeply.[5]

And further Calvin adds:

> As therefore our capacity cannot endure the fullness of the infinite glory which belongs to the essence of God, it is necessary whenever He appears to us that He put on a form adapted to our capacity . . . but as I already said, we ought not to imagine God in His essence to be like any appearance to His own prophet and other holy fathers, but He continually puts on various appearances, according to man's comprehension, to whom He wished to give some signs of His presence.[6]

[5] *Institutes* I.v.9.
[6] *Commentary on Daniel* 7:9, quoted by Dowey, *op. cit.*, pp. 12–13.

Judging from the many quotations put together by T. F. Torrance from the whole range of Calvin's writings,[7] his conception of divine accommodation appears to be discussed in two ways. On the one hand, there is the fact that all of our knowledge of God is analogical. That is, it is conveyed by words which point to things familiar to us, "for God cannot reveal Himself to us in any other way than by comparison with things which we know."[8]

On the other hand, Calvin puts no faith in reason, or in man's natural ability unaided by the Spirit, to come to an adequate knowledge of God.

> And this was the original source of idolatry, that men supposed they could not otherwise possess God unless by subjecting Him to their own imagination. Nothing, however, can be more preposterous; for since the minds of men and all their senses sink far below the loftiness of God, when they try to bring Him down to the measure of their own weak capacity, they travesty Him. In a word, whatever man's reason conceives of Him is mere falsehood; nevertheless, this depraved longing can hardly be repressed, so fiercely does it burst out.[9]

Man on his own resources, in other words, is a remarkable creator of idols.

To avoid the danger of idolatry in image-making Calvin appears to make a number of assertions, all of which are grounded in a high conception of revelation in the Bible, and also on the experience of faith. Thus, our knowledge of God must correspond to God's initiative as revealed in his Word. To embrace the Scriptures with reverence and expectation leads one to obedience, "for not only does faith, full and perfect faith, but *all correct knowledge of God, originate in obedience.*"[10] This is not simply a human doing. Simply reading the external Word is in itself to no avail unless it is made

---

[7] *Calvin's Doctrine of Man* (Grand Rapids: Wm. B. Eerdmans Publishing Co., 1957), esp. pp. 128–153.

[8] *Commentary on Isaiah* 40:18.

[9] *Commentary on Exodus* 32:1, *Harmony,* Vol. III (Grand Rapids: Wm. B. Eerdmans Publishing Co., 1950), p. 330.

[10] *Institutes* I.6.2.

alive by the power of the Spirit of God. Thus, God through the Spirit works with the Word within us to confirm and empower it.[11] Finally, God prevents us from mere idol-making or mere imaginative speculation by providing us with an image of his own choosing, Jesus Christ, who is the supreme example of God's making himself little for us, of his accommodation to our needs.[12]

Dowey insists that even the incarnation of God in Christ, however, refers not so much to the essence of God as to the manner in which he makes himself known to us. Calvin's principle of accommodation, then, presents a boundary beyond which he will not go even in his Christology.[13] T. F. Torrance has added to this point the observation that Calvin showed the greatest restraint when he spoke of Christ's incarnation and ascension in regard to space and time.

> The ascension, for example, must be stated in a thoroughly realistic way in accordance with the human nature of the incarnate Son and its involvement in the space and time of our world, yet because we are concerned here with an act of God that transcends expression in language tied down to space and time, the statement, in sheer faithfulness to what is indicated, breaks off and points infinitely beyond itself, beyond even the "heaven of heavens," as Calvin put it. It belongs to Calvin's great merit that he saw that in the nature of the case we are unable to convey in statements how statements are related to the realities they point to; if we think we can do that we are only substituting statements for realities.

Torrance claims that when this basic distinction is not made, the acts of God are so subjected "to our notions of space and time that they become mythologized in our understanding and then require demythologizing. This is very apparent in the theologies of Bult-

---

[11] See Arthur A. Hays, "The Ultimate Basis for the Authority of Scripture According to Calvin," *From the Pyramids to Paul* (ed. by L. G. Leary, G. L. Robinson *Festschrift;* New York: Thomas Nelson and Sons, 1935), pp. 79–94.

[12] See T. F. Torrance, *op. cit.*, pp. 135–136.

[13] So Dowey, *op. cit.*, pp. 14–17.

mann and Tillich, both of which are based on a rejection" of
Calvin's position, which early Lutheran theologians nicknamed
extra Calvinisticum."[14]

Paul Tillich, more than any other in our time, has articulated a
carefully reasoned view of the religious symbol and sees the task
of theology as dealing critically with the received religious symbols.[15] I cannot see the ground of Torrance's ranging Tillich beside
Bultmann in his statement just quoted. Tillich believed that his definition of God by means of the depth dimension as "the ground of
being" was as near a nonsymbolic statement as one could make. To
what degree this is the case has been debated, but in any event all
theology beyond this deals in symbols.[16] Bultmann's program, on
the other hand, based on his contrast between religious and scientific man,[17] begins in his demythologizing of the New Testament
with a proper consideration of the hermeneutical problem which the
New Testament world view presents. Yet he ends with the virtual
desymbolization of New Testament language. Thus, to place him
with Tillich as foil for Calvin's view of accommodation is not a
particularly successful procedure.

For Tillich the chief criterion of the symbol is that the Unconditioned is clearly grasped in its unconditionedness. The Unconditioned is symbolized in "the source of both existence and meaning,

[14] "Calvin and the Knowledge of God," *The Christian Century,* May
27, 1964, pp. 696–699. For a special study of the *extra Calvinisticum,*
see E. David Willis, *Calvin's Catholic Christology (Studies in Medieval
and Reformation Thought,* Vol. II; Leiden: E. J. Brill, 1966).

[15] See Tillich's "The Religious Symbol" (an article originally pub-
lished in 1928 in German, tr. by James Luther Adams, assisted by
Ernst Fraenkel), *The Journal of Liberal Religion,* Vol. II (1940), pp.
13–33; reprinted in Rollo May, ed., *Symbolism in Religion and Liter-
ature* (New York: George Braziller, 1960), pp. 75–98. Also, "Religious
Symbols and Our Knowledge of God," *The Christian Scholar,* Vol.
XXXVIII (1955), pp. 189–197; and *Systematic Theology,* Vol. I
(Chicago: University of Chicago Press, 1951), pp. 238–244, 286–289.

[16] *Systematic Theology,* Vol. I, p. 239.

[17] Both are rather artificial and unreal categories. At best one must
say that such abstractions as "religious man" and "scientific man" can
be no more than subcultures in man's overall image of the world, the
basic framework of which is sociopolitical.

which transcends being-in-itself as well as being-for-us." The trouble has been that the symbols themselves, or the ultimate mystery being symbolized, lose their real nature, become objectified, and thus conceal the Unconditioned, or the ground of our being. This objectification leads to loss of power in the symbol and obscuring of the true nature of the Ultimate to which it points. The figurative quality of the symbol implies an inner attitude which does not have the symbol itself in view but a greater reality which is invisible or transcendent but which becomes apprehended in the symbol now.

Tillich distinguishes several elements which make up the meaning of the term "symbol" as used in his theology:

1. Symbols differ from signs in that the latter do not participate in the reality and power of that to which they point. Symbols, on the other hand, "although they are not the same as that which they symbolize, participate in its meaning and power." A letter of the alphabet as written points to a sound but does not participate in it. "On the other hand, the flag participates in the power of the king or the nation for which it stands and which it symbolizes."[18]

2. "Every symbol opens up a level of reality for which non-symbolic speaking is inadequate." ". . . every symbol is two-edged. It opens up reality and it opens up the soul."

3. Religious symbols do exactly what all symbols do; "they open up a level of reality, which otherwise is not opened at all, which is hidden. I would call this the depth dimension of reality itself, the dimension of reality which is the ground of every other dimension and every other depth, and which therefore is not on one level beside the others but is the fundamental level, the level below all other levels, the level of being itself, or the ultimate power of being. . . . The dimension of ultimate reality is the dimension of the Holy. And so we can also say, religious symbols are symbols of the Holy."

4. There are two fundamental levels in all religious symbols: "the transcendent level, the level which goes *beyond* the empirical reality we encounter, and the immanent level, the level which we

[18] This and the other three points below with the quotations are taken from the article, "Religious Symbols and Our Knowledge of God," *op. cit.* (see n. 15), pp. 189–195.

find *within* the encounter of reality." The second is "the level of the appearances of the divine in time and space." In the famous discussion between Luther and Zwingli, held in Marburg in 1529, "Luther wanted to maintain the genuinely symbolic character of the elements, but Zwingli said that the sacramental materials, bread and wine, are 'only symbolic.' Thus Zwingli meant that they are only signs pointing to a story of the past. Even in that period there was semantic confusion. And let us not be misled by this. In the real sense of symbol, the sacramental materials are symbols. But if the symbol is used as *only* symbol (i.e., only signs), then of course the sacramental materials are more than this."

Both Dowey and Torrance claim that Calvin's views of God's accommodation are something very different from what is referred to as "a symbolic conception of religious knowledge." For both the problem of symbols, or in the words of Torrance "thinking in pictures," refers to language we create, what we consider to be the most adequate to picture the Unknown. For Calvin, on the other hand, the symbols are part of the structure of God's self-revelation. They are the way God would have us know him as God.

For Calvin, furthermore, the use of images is proper but only in the sense that they point beyond themselves to a Reality that cannot be pictured. "Theological language," says Torrance, "is thus deeply analogical but not mythological." Images of the mind may be idols, because the God so imagined cannot be materialized within our senses. The habit of thinking in pictures is for Torrance dangerous because the pictures become mythology which must be demythologized. Calvin's principle of accommodation is claimed to take a different route and avoid this danger. To the extent that Calvin accorded a much higher value to the Bible as revelation than did Tillich, this critique of Tillich is no doubt true. Yet there is a danger in overstating the point and becoming involved in a semantic discussion of terms. For neither Calvin nor Tillich is "thinking in pictures" an end in itself, but only a kind of bridge between our finitude and the infinite which is not in itself a symbol. Unless the symbol points to that which is so much greater than itself that it cannot otherwise be talked about, it is not a proper religious symbol. Torrance's objection is certainly valid against Bultmann, but it must be considerably rephrased before it sufficiently states the radical difference between Calvin and Tillich.

III

The essential point for both Calvin and Tillich, that the symbols to be genuine must bear a vital inner relation to ultimate reality and are not simply products of clever minds, can be illustrated from the world of physical reality. Here scientists have long had a problem with the question of what light is. On the one side, the propagation of light has been proposed as undulatory, a mechanical or electromagnetic wave motion. Light can be interfered with, stopped from proceeding further, or it can be diffracted or polarized. These properties are comprehensible if light is a wave, but not comprehensible if light is a series of particles because two particles cannot destroy each other. Finally, light does not possess an intrinsic mass. It has energy and movement but one evidently cannot weigh it.[19]

On the other hand, another series of observations suggests that light is corpuscular, the corpuscles being named photons. For example, the photoelectric effect of light has a natural explanation in the photon hypothesis. When light falls upon a metal surface, electrons are found to jump out from the surface in a random fashion and not such as one would assume from a steady wave. Now, if light itself consisted of darts in photon fashion, and if they were distributed at random in the light band, then the electrons of the metal would indeed emerge chaotically as they were struck by the photon darts. Another example, called the *Compton Effect*, seems to deal the wave theory a final blow. Once a wave exists, it simply cannot change its frequency. It can change velocity, and direction can be altered, but not quantity. Yet in 1923 Compton

[19] For the discussion of this point and those in the following two paragraphs, see Henry Margenau, *The Nature of Physical Reality* (New York: McGraw-Hill, 1950), pp. 307 ff.

showed that material objects scattering X rays altered their frequency. If, then, a *corpuscle* of light collides with a material particle, it has less energy after the collision. "Thus light appears as a swarm of particles and behaves like particles in collision with other particles of matter."

The same ambivalence is true regarding an electron. It has properties of both particles and waves. Yet the properties of the two are antithetical. Is what is basic to nature then dualistic? Professor Margenau of Yale, whose work I have been summarizing, simply says that an electron is neither wave nor particle. Those terms become metaphorical when applied to it; the heart of nature remains intrinsically uncertain with respect to the terms we have to use in ordinary speech. "The physicist, in order to grasp reality, has had cause to heed the counsel: Thou shalt not make unto thee any graven image." A mechanical conception of nature, for example, to which the physical particle notion inevitably leads, is always threatened with catastrophe. As an ultimate mode of understanding, it is, therefore, "predestined to be inadequate." Hence, from the very beginning one cardinal fact, says Margenau, has to be recognized: "The uncertainty of the immediately given." Not even "such basic qualities as position in space and time [can be shown] to be universally meaningful."[20]

Werner Heisenberg has made the following observations about the nature of knowledge in physics:

> . . . we are finally led to believe that the laws of nature which we formulate mathematically in quantum theory deal no longer with the particles themselves but with our knowledge of the elementary particles. The question whether these particles exist in space and time "in themselves" can thus no longer be posed in this form. We can only talk about the processes that occur when, through the interaction of the particle with some other physical system such as a measuring instrument, the behavior of the particle is to be disclosed. The conception of the objective reality of the elementary particles has thus evaporated in a curious way, not into the fog of some new, obscure, or not yet understood reality concept, but into the transparent

[20] *Ibid.,* pp. 322–323.

clarity of a mathematics that represents no longer the behavior of the elementary particles but rather our knowledge of this behavior. The atomic physicist has had to come to terms with the fact that his science is only a link in the endless chain of discussions of man with nature, but that it cannot simply talk of nature "as such." Natural science presupposes man, and we must become aware of the fact that . . . we are not only spectators but also always participants on the stage of life.[21]

Here again analogies are posed for the theologian. Ultimate reality of the physical sciences cannot be grasped in and for itself. It only discloses itself to the one searching for it by some measuring or other device which he has constructed. What is pictured is a human relation to natural process, knowledge which is this side of the ultimate itself. ". . . the Cartesian differentiation of *res cogitans* and *res extensa* [subjective and objective things] is no longer suitable as the starting point for the understanding of modern science."[22]

Note the following corroboration of points in our discussion about God:

1. The nature of the ultimate reality, whether it be the physical components of the universe or the source of ultimate power and meaning, is simply not known. What it is in itself is beyond our comprehension. Yet we do know something of how the basic components of nature relate to each other. Our knowledge is often contradictory and dialectical, and it is always partial.

2. The ultimate component reveals itself in our searching. It reveals that it is, not what it is, and its revelation is by accommodation to our limitations. Hence, the words we use point to it, and speak truth about it, but only limited portions of the whole truth. Yet reality and our words about it bear an inner authentic relation. Though limited and pointing beyond themselves to what

[21] "The Representation of Nature in Contemporary Physics," *Symbolism in Religion and Literature* (ed. by Rollo May), pp. 215–232 (quote from p. 221). This reference was given me by James Luther Adams.
[22] *Ibid.*, p. 231.

cannot be entirely known or verbalized by us, our words are not a completely artificial concoction.

IV

It is the nature of human cognition, therefore, that it knows only in part. Between the knower and the ultimate stands our own finitude. We cannot get to Reality directly, except through a mediation in which the unexpressible accommodates itself to our expression. Only by revelation, then, can we speak and know.

It has been the argument of these chapters that the new Reality of which the Bible bears witness reveals its truth in its own way. The form of the revelation is in event, in dialogue as one form of event, in special newsworthy happenings which can be located for the most part in time and space. The very form, then, prevents the religion from becoming a philosophy. Instead, the outcome is a people whose historical activity has at the center faith and trust in the Faithful One, praise in the grace of God to whom the proper response is a love which is loyal service and obedience in the whole of the people's life.

By what models of understanding can this type of self-knowledge be apprehended, given the fact that the source of human action is not by pure idea but by experienced events which serve as symbols to inspire, interpret, and organize the self? Obviously dominant is the purposeful organization of world order, the concept of power behind the order, moving to save man from his self-destruction and the misuse of his freedom and power of self by acts of will. As an agent whose grateful service for unmerited benefit was expected, a special people was brought into being. How can these basic elements of self-understanding be portrayed powerfully? The Bible unquestionably did it politically, the known goodness of God purifying and purging the symbols used. The Divine Suzerain, therefore, is the purified ideal of what the earthly suzerain should be. And the power inherent in the Suzerain is directed toward the universal rule of God which when acknowledged by all will mean universal peace. The Divine Ruler uses his power for the salvation of a creation that exists in violation of its origin.

Now if one objects that such language is not usable by those who live in a democracy, let it be remembered that democracy rests on a Biblically oriented view of man as sinner for whom power is a dangerous thing because it corrupts him. Therefore, the powers of a society of people, carefully distributed to check and balance one another, is the only system of things that can be expected to produce the largest measure of justice. Democracy is the creation of a long period of struggle because human, earthly monarchs proved inadequate to their task, misusing the powers seized or granted by them. The Biblical image of cosmic government is the personification of the good, the ideal in man's ancient system of government.

Christ's center of attention was clearly the divine *basileia,* or Kingdom, and the role he had been sent to play in its introduction and consummation. Is there any place in the Bible, then, where the conception is not central or does not stand as background giving the foreground its setting and meaning? I am unable to discover such a place, except where God is not the major subject or background as, for example, in Esther and the Song of Songs. The scholar may insist, therefore, that if the sense of cosmic government, revealed to Israel, and the Hebrew grasping of God's reality through the form of Suzerain, were to be considered a mythology inappropriate to our use, then there remains nothing to which the language of the Bible points or in which it has its setting. The Bible would possess nothing for us but sayings, beautiful moralisms, fine literature, excellent narration, but it would present no claim upon us to love as we have been loved, to obey him who would save us from ourselves, and to have the same mind in us as was in him.

Following Calvin's principle of accommodation, or Tillich's picture of the role of the religious symbol, then, we can affirm that the Biblical Divine Monarch points, not to what the ultimately real or the ground of meaning is in itself, but to the manner in which the Bible's God would have us know him as God, for only so does he identify for us who we are and how we are to live.

The Canon as Theological Problem

IN THE preceding chapters a conscious attempt has been made not only to present certain Old Testament material within the context of recent research, but at the same time to avoid bibliolatrous statements. The history of Biblical interpretation clearly indicates that intellectuals in western culture have rarely held the view that simply because a thing is Biblical it must be accepted as bald prose of automatic efficacy in the current scene. The problem instead has been how it is to be interpreted in a new and different historical environment than that of which it was originally a part. That is, what is God saying to us now in the words of the ancient literature? To answer that question properly would involve much of the history of western theology, whether Jewish or Christian.

This means that there is something to the term "Scripture," that is, to the conception of a special body of literature set apart from other literatures. Theologians who in their conscious work in theology give only a passing glance at the subject of the canon of Scripture nevertheless will quote from it, or allude to it as from a special literature, something especially set apart. My colleague, Harvey Cox, is commonly associated with the "new left" in theology. In his *The Secular City*,[1] however, he takes particular delight in quoting from the Bible to support his case. Indeed, the book seems to operate on an axiom that if something is reasonable in itself, and can be supported by something from the Bible, particularly from the Old Testament, it is clearly correct. Senator Everett M. Dirksen is quoted as having once said: "Any politician who is to get anywhere in this country must first get right with Lincoln!" So it is

[1] New York: The Macmillan Company, 1965.

with most theologians with regard to the Bible. On one occasion or another, nearly all of them, no matter their type of theologizing, will have sought to give the impression that they are right with the Bible!

Also in the preceding chapters a view of the Bible as Scripture, as a literature possessing special significance for western culture, has been implied throughout, though never discussed. At the outset the question was asked: Accepting a high view of the Old Testament as an integral part of Scripture, what are some basic consequences for theology? Now in the book's final chapter we must ask about the theological problem of the conception of the canon so far taken for granted. How are we to view this subject in the context of contemporary research? The question will be dealt with on two levels: First, a formal question as to the reason for a fixed or closed canon; and, second, the more practical question as to how the Bible has actually been used by synagogue and church. The answer to the second question should reveal what the canon of Scripture is in actual practice. A concluding question will concern the canon as here defined and the question of its truth.

I

An initial question, frequently asked, is to this writer not a serious problem. It may be phrased somewhat as follows: "If God is the living God, the God of Abraham, Moses, Isaiah, Ezra, and the Father of Jesus Christ, who through the Holy Spirit still works his signs and wonders in our midst, why is there a closed canon? How can it ever be closed? Is not the Creator eternally creating, and the Sovereign actively ruling in our midst?"

One brief answer is that history has long since decided the issue. The Bible is simply a fact. It exists as a given body of literature which comes to us from the generations of our fathers, who in turn preserved it from the ruins of antiquity. Theologically, one could say that its creation and existence are an act of God. In any event it simply is. If today one wishes to learn of the classical rootage of Judaism and Christianity, it is to this literature that one must turn, not to the Koran, nor to the Hindu or Buddhist Scriptures.

To one who asks why certain other books should not be included, one must counter with the question as to what books? Shall we omit Esther and put in 1–2 Maccabees, or omit James and include the Didache, or Teaching (of the Twelve Apostles)? Yet what would be changed? If the debates about marginal books in antiquity should all be resolved today in favor of the marginal, little would be different. Protestants at the Reformation opted for the Palestinian canon, omitting a group of books included in the Alexandrian canon which is that of the Roman Catholic Church. If this decision were today reversed so that all Christians held to the Alexandrian canon, what would be changed? No major theologians today, whether Protestant or Catholic, would base any central issue for faith or life on material contained solely in a marginal book. The Bible possesses great variety, but its major books are acknowledged by all to create the real canon, while the marginal books are studied largely for historical developments because they are generally later than the basic or really creative works.

Or another question is asked. Why not include some of the great devotional literature of the ages, such as the writings of Thomas à Kempis and the prayers of St. Francis of Assisi? To me the normative answer for our generation has been given by H. Richard Niebuhr in his small classic, *The Meaning of Revelation.*[2] Niebuhr states quite simply that the later literature is to be explained and interpreted by the Bible, but not the other way around. The later exists because the Bible preceded it and created the movement and the devotional milieu of which the subsequent literature is a part. And as to the Bible's authority, that will remain in some measure as long as there is a community with a history that traces its origin to events of which the Bible bears witness. It will remain as long as portions of it, at least, are regarded as testimony to the creative origin of the faith which the community espouses.

This fact of the Bible's existence means that it is an objective and formal standard for Christians, at least, and for Jews also in the sense that the Old Testament contains the revealed Torah to-

[2] New York: The Macmillan Company, 1941.

gether with a special group of sacred writings gathered around it. Though there seems no need to discuss the point further for my present purpose, it should not be neglected in the discussion to follow. It furnishes the sole context for, the chief limiting factor in, the discussion of canon from the standpoint of usage.

II

One of the chief problems of the Biblical scholar today is that of the unity of the Bible. What modern research has been increasingly emphasizing about both the Old and New Testaments is the extraordinary variety of material and viewpoint within them both. The question is more urgent than ever before as to what, if anything, holds the literature together as a guide or standard for any subsequent time. If such a guide or standard exists, is it to be found in the literature itself, or is it to be found outside the canon to which the latter is bound? Clearly, both descriptive and dogmatic concerns have always been present, and the illustrations provided in Chapter 2 suggest their presence in our own work today. Yet before proceeding further with this question, let us turn to a brief examination of the nature of the Scriptural variety.

Biblical tradition, whether as text transmission or as history of the great traditions of the people, was a developing tradition. The fixing of the canon seems to have been almost an artificial cutting off of something alive, evolving, moving, like an organism.

Scholars tell us, for example, that the doxology at the end of the Lord's Prayer is a liturgical addition, added to form a fitting conclusion and climax to the prayer by Christians who were using it regularly in services of worship. The Revised Standard Version has a footnote at the end of the prayer in Matthew 6:13: "Other authorities, some ancient, add, in some form, *'For thine is the kingdom and the power and the glory, forever. Amen.'* " The translators of the Authorized or King James Version left these words in the text. Those of the RSV relegated them to a footnote because the study of the text's transmission strongly suggests that they were not in the original gospel. The last twelve verses of the Gospel of Mark

(16:9–20) are also omitted from the text of RSV and placed in a footnote for the same reason.

Is there not a canonical principle implied in these two examples from RSV's footnotes; namely, that only the most primitive portions of the Gospels can be considered canonical or really Scriptural? Yet the verses alluded to were added from oral tradition by believers to their manuscripts so that ultimately they became part of the normative text tradition. Modern Biblical scholarship has attempted to excise certain glosses or additions which can more or less clearly be detected. But should we not openly confess that our putting verses 9–20 of Mark 16 into fine print, so that they will not be used in the churches, rests upon a kind of primitivism which supposes that only the original words of the Gospel are to be considered Scriptural? Can we longer be quite sure that we ever can establish precisely what the original text was?

This illustration is given, not to find fault with the RSV, but only to suggest that Protestant scholars in particular have not always been explicit about the canonical implications of their work. A previous generation believed it possible by textual and literary critical work to detect all glosses to the text so that the original could be reconstructed. When the actual words of the prophets and Jesus were recovered, we presumably would have had the authoritative record to be used in our time. Yet it is realized by all now that this primitivistic ideal cannot be attained.

At the opposite pole from such views is the canonical presupposition behind the recent translation of the *Torah* (Gen.—Deut.), published in 1962 by the Jewish Publication Society. Professor Harry M. Orlinsky, chairman of the translation committee and one of the leading text critics of our time, felt he could not do in that translation for the Jewish community what he had been doing in his many contributions to the discipline of text criticism. Instead it was felt necessary to attempt a translation of the Masoretic Text, that is, of the received or traditional text, as it has been preserved in the tradition.[3] That means that the text critical work of the rab-

---

[3] "The New Jewish Version of the Torah," *Journal of Biblical Literature,* Vol. LXXXII (1963), pp. 249–264, esp. 260–264. See also

binical authorities in the early centuries of our era is taken as normative for the Jewish people.

The text criticism of the Biblical manuscripts found since 1947 in caves along the cliffs of the western shores of the Dead Sea have illumined in more detail what is implied by that position. Frank M. Cross, Jr. especially has made a very strong case for the position that three primary text traditions can be detected in this material. One is the Palestinian, often called Proto-Lucianic from a group of manuscripts that are in a tradition followed by the early Christian scholar, Lucian of Antioch (died *ca.* A.D. 312). Texts in this tradition are quoted, for example, by the Chronicler (in 1–2 Chron., Ezra, and Neh.), by the early Jewish historian Josephus, and by various authors of New Testament books.

A second text tradition at Qumran is Egyptian. It is to be found in Hebrew texts which can be reconstructed from the Septuagint, the Greek translation made in Egypt during the third and second centuries B.C. The third text tradition is the Masoretic, or the received text which rabbinic authorities have regarded as normative. By hypothesis Professor Cross cogently argues that this must derive from the Babylonian community of rabbinic learning. In any case, when Jewish scholars during the first century A.D. decided to take action to form a text which would be regarded as normative by all Jewish communities, they did not attempt to construct a conflate edition, made by taking the "best" readings from the various text traditions. Instead, they chose one tradition, the Babylonian, for most of the Old Testament and discarded the others. This is suggested by the fact that all known manuscripts of the second century A.D. are Masoretic in type. The variety in Hebrew manuscripts ceases and is preserved to some extent only in the translations.[4]

Orlinsky's important article on "The Textual Criticism of the Old Testament," *The Bible and the Ancient Near East* (ed. by G. E. Wright; Garden City, N.Y.: Doubleday Anchor Books, 1965, originally published in 1961), pp. 140–169.

[4] See esp. Frank M. Cross, Jr., The History of the Biblical Text in the Light of the Discoveries in the Judean Desert," *Harvard Theological Review,* Vol. 57 (1964), pp. 281–299; and "The Contribution of the Qumrân Discoveries to the Study of the Biblical Text," *Israel*

Yet the first appearance now known of the Babylonian text-type in the "Former Prophets" (Josh.—2 Kings) is already a conflate tradition in what is called the Proto-Theodotion family or Old Greek translation. In any case, Cross maintains that the Masoretic Text as we know it came into being between the era of Hillel and the first Jewish revolt (A.D. 66–70). He says:

The principles which guided the scholars who prepared the recension were unusual. The recension was not characterized by wholesale revision and emendation, nor by eclectic or conflating procedures. Nor was a single, local textual family chosen. In the Pentateuch the current Palestinian text-type was rejected, and along with it the Palaeo-Hebrew script and orthographic innovations that marked certain of its exemplars. Rather the conservative, superb text of Babylonian origin, recently introduced into Palestine, was selected for the standard text. In the Former Prophets, the same pattern was followed, a Babylonian text was chosen, despite the existence of the superior Old Palestinian textual family. Presumably the pattern was set by the selection of the Pentateuch. In the Latter Prophets, the scholars shifted textual families. In these books a Palestinian text was chosen, perhaps because Babylonian texts were not available. However that may be, the orthographic type chosen was not the new *plene* style common in many Palestinian manuscripts beginning in Maccabaean times.

The process of recension was basically one of selecting traditions deriving from two old textual families available in Palestine in the first century A.D.

There was some leveling through, not always successful, of the conservative orthographic style chosen, and some revision, within narrow limits, was undertaken. The process was not

---

Exploration Journal, Vol. 16 (1966), pp. 81–95. A text critic working within the framework of Jewish Orthodoxy will, of course, maintain a normative character for the Masoretic tradition all along, a position which Cross claims the evidence does not support (so "The Contribution of Qumrân . . . ," pp. 90–93).

evolutionary or adventitious, but one of careful selection between sharply differing traditions. It was in short a systematic if not radical process of recension.[5]

This requires the view that in the midst of the development of the various text traditions, a choice had finally to be made by a more or less *ad hoc* human decision. Of course it is rare indeed that a text critical problem involves a serious theological issue. Great issues for faith and life seldom revolve around the translation or meaning of a single Biblical text. Nevertheless, the point at issue is clear: A rich variety in a developing tradition is suddenly limited or cut off by the community which is attempting to preserve the tradition.

III

What appears to be true in text transmission is more vividly present in the history of the tradition. Research on the Dead Sea Scrolls and on Intertestamental history has forced upon us different conclusions about several issues than were held by the generation on whose shoulders we stand. The Psalms Scroll of Cave 11, for example, actually preserves some Maccabean (2nd cent. B.C.) psalms. Their type of composition is almost a patchwork quilt of quotations from canonical psalms.[6] This is only one of many pieces of evidence which lead us to the hypothesis that by about 400 B.C., or by the early fourth century, the idea of an authoritative Old Testament literature was present and was generally fixed as to main outlines in the historical traditions and in the collection of prophets, hymns, and wisdom material in Psalms, Proverbs, and Job. There were marginal books that for long were debated. Finally, Palestinian rabbis accepted only four from the marginal list: the Song of Songs, Esther, Ecclesiastes, and Daniel. Egyptian rabbis earlier had committed themselves during the third and second centuries B.C. to a longer list which included among other things the stories of the

[5] *Ibid.*, pp. 94–95.
[6] See Jim A. Sanders, *The Psalms Scroll of Qumrân Cave 11 (11QPs^a)*, (*Discoveries in the Judean Desert*, Vol. 4; Oxford: Clarendon Press, 1965); and *The Dead Sea Psalms Scroll* (New York: Cornell University Press, 1967).

Maccabean wars in 1–2 Maccabees. Palestinian rabbis rejected them for what they obviously felt was more ancient material. As previously stated, therefore, the cut-off point in the marginal literature was in the end an *ad hoc* decision of the community.

In handling the historical material today many of us are heavily influenced by the arguments of Martin Noth to the effect that there are just three great collections of historical traditon: The Tetrateuch (Gen.–Num.), the Deuteronomic History of Israel in the Promised Land (Deut.–2 Kings), and the Chronicler's History of Judah for the small postexilic community (1–2 Chron., Ezra, and Neh.).

The first or Tetrateuch is the Jerusalem priesthood's (designated P's) exilic or early postexilic edition of the old epic (JE). In the transmission of the epic, the earliest stages cannot be unraveled with any certainty.[7] The first written edition of it which can be detected, labeled *J,* is now generally dated to the tenth century B.C., and attributed to someone in the court of David and Solomon in Jerusalem. A series of additions to J with special theological tendencies lead to the hypothesis that another written history existed alongside J. It is given the symbol *E,* and its composition in written form is dated to the late tenth or early ninth century. Because of this tradition's interest in the office of prophecy and in the tradition of the Mosaic Covenant over against the developing theology of the Davidic covenant in Jerusalem, it is assumed that E must represent the traditions of North Israel's Levites and prophets. Yet it must be stressed that we do not possess E except as a series of additions to J, the basic work.[8] They must have been added to J after the

---

[7] This is essentially what John Bright is saying in his protest against the methodology of Martin Noth's *Überlieferungsgeschichte des Pentateuch* (Stuttgart: W. Kohlhammer Verlag, 1948). See Bright's monograph, *Early Israel in Recent History Writing* (*Studies in Biblical Theology,* No. 19; London: SCM Press, and Naperville, Ill., Alec Allenson, 1956).

[8] For a contemporary treatment in detail, the Harvard dissertation of Alan W. Jenks, "The Elohist and North Israelite Traditions" (1965) elaborates these views. The conception of J as the basic document is taken with Noth and von Rad from P. Volz and W. Rudolph, *Der Elohist als Erzähler: Ein Irrweg der Pentateuchkritik? (Beitrage zur*

fall of the northern kingdom to the Assyrians in 722–721 B.C. The remainder of E, not preserved, must have been so close to what J has that it was not necessary to add more. These close similarities in the two traditions require the assumption of an earlier work (G from the German *Grundschrift*), whether oral or written is unknown, behind them both, going back into the Tribal League.

At the end of the seventh century B.C. the Deuteronomic historian (Dtr.) appears to have compiled the bulk of the History of Israel in the Promised Land, using and quoting from many sources, not preserved. It is a theological history, defending the justice of the ways of God to Israel in the clashes of empire building during the first millennium B.C. His key to understanding is the divine promise of the land to the Patriarchs, a promise made conditional upon faithful observance of the Mosiac covenant. The central theme for the interpretation of what happened was God's maintenance of covenant in spite of Israel's repeated violations, his punishment for breach to treaty until finally North Israel fell to the Assyrians. The theology of the work seems to have been North Israelite in origin, and the core of the old Book of Deuteronomy (perhaps Deut. 5–28), seems to have been used as the basis upon which the history was erected. The reform of Josiah (622 B.C.) seems to have been based on the old book and represented the first reform in Jerusalem occasioned by the northern theology. Perhaps another member of the same theological group brought the work up to date (*ca.* 560–550 B.C.), following the fall of Jerusalem.

This Dtr. history work seems to have been known and preserved during the Babylonian Exile. The Jerusalem priests also preserved archival material from the temple, and during the early Exile they edited the JE epic in such a way as to preserve what they considered essential in Genesis through Numbers.

When Ezra as Commissioner for Jewish Affairs in the Persian government returned to Palestine during the third quarter of the fifth century B.C., he was empowered to reform religious conditions

---

Wissenschaft von Alten und Neuen Testament 63 [1933]; Giessen: Töpelmann, 1963); and W. Rudolph, *Der Elohist von Exodus bis Josua* (BZAW 68 [1938]). See Martin Noth's assessment in *Überlieferungsgeschichte des Pentateuch*, pp. 20–44,

according to "the law [or wisdom] of God which is in your hand" (Ezra 7:14, 25). Scholars almost unanimiously have taken this to mean that Ezra was returning with the Pentateuch completed in its final form, so that it could be used as constitutional law, the Torah of Moses, for the Jerusalem community, implying that it was also so used already in Babylonia.

Finally, not far from *ca.* 400 B.C., the Chronicler drew on 1–2 Samuel, 1–2 Kings, and upon independent sources, whether written or oral, or both, we do not know, to write the history of Judah for the surviving community. The threat of community dissolution for treaty violation had seen fruition in the fall of Jerusalem. What now must be held to for survival was the divine commitment to (or covenant with) David. Hence the figure of David is held up before the new community as an ideal, and God's covenant with David is an anchor of hope for a future of fulfilled promises.

Yet at this point the historical tradition breaks off. In Palestine at least Holy Writ recounted the Restoration through Ezra and then rapidly was cut off. A richly developing tradition in which past kerygma is repeatedly reassessed in various ways for its contemporary message is suddenly halted and determined to be canonically complete.

IV

Helmut H. Koester has recently cited with approval the statement of J. Schniewind that one can only understand the origin of the Gospels in the New Testament and any forms of Christian literature which preceded them on the supposition that there was a kerygma which proclaimed that a man who once lived "in the flesh" is the "Lord." This belief and proclamation of the early Christian community is what "has made the written Gospel a distinctive type of written literature. It can be most clearly seen in the Gospel of Mark, which is nothing but a passion narrative with biographical introduction."[9]

[9] "One Jesus and Four Primitive Gospels," *Harvard Theological Review,* Vol. 61.2 (April, 1968), p. 206. My remarks about New Testament tradition are dependent upon Koester's most creative article, and a second cited in n. 13.

In the exceedingly complex process by which New Testament traditions evolved it is possible to speak of the oldest oral tradition that preceded any written sources, of written documents intermediate between the oral stage and written gospels, of a variety of gospels which both preceded and followed the canonical gospels, and of the four gospels, Matthew, Mark, Luke, and John, which were selected out of a great mass of literature as normative expressions of the Church's belief and faith in Christ as Lord.

In this evolving literature Koester points to certain types of writing which left their mark on the canonical tradition. One of these is collections of the sayings of Jesus. They must have served a great variety of purpose in the preaching, teaching, and worship of the church. Matthew and Luke appear to have used one such sayings source which scholars have labeled "Q." A full development of this type of literature is the second-century Gospel of Thomas where a great variety of sayings, only loosely connected to one another, are presented without any relation to the life of Jesus. It was sufficient that Jesus said this or that. The eschatological expectation of the Kingdom in Jesus' canonical teaching is here transformed from future event to a hidden secret which is present and to be discovered, a hidden treasure which one must find in the words of Jesus and in oneself.[10]

Another type of source must have contained miracle stories for the most part, the purpose of which was to exalt Christ as the Divine Man. The Gospels of Mark and John evidently used one such source wherein Jesus appears as one endowed with the power of God to perform miracles which in turn prove the divine presence in his life. Both Mark and John used this source critically by emphasizing Jesus' death on the cross. Yet other early Christians, as Paul's letters reveal, were very successful in their proclamations of a Christ who transcended all limitations of human life. "What Paul calls the 'Christ according to the flesh' (2 Cor. 5:16) was for his opponents the divine man Jesus whose glorious deeds were remembered and constituted the central 'Christological' material of their religious convictions.'"[11] The influence of the conception carried

[10] *Ibid.*, pp. 213–221.

[11] *Ibid.*, p. 234. See also Dieter Georgi, *Die Gegner des Paulus im*

over into an emphasis on the miraculous deeds of the apostles and missionaries which is seen in its most vivid expression in the Apocryphal Acts of the Apostles.

The apocalyptic viewpoint that forms a substratum to the teaching of Jesus and the acts of the apostles was briefly summarized in Chapter 5. This is related to, or drawn from, what apparently was a great mass of both Jewish and Christian apocalyptic material. A secondary stage in this tradition, according to Koester, is the collection of teachings of Jesus to his disciples placed between his public ministry and before his passion (cf. Mark 13 and John 13–17). Not included in the canon are the oldest Christian "revelations" preserved: the Apocalypse of John and the Shepherd of Hermas. A further development in the type will be certain Gnostic gospels, following the pattern of teaching to the disciples, usually on a mountain, in which the eschatological element is eliminated for secrets or mysteries being revealed to the uninitiated.[12]

Out of all such material and much more one may well wonder how the four gospels preserved as canonical came to be selected and accepted as such. While usage was one factor of importance, there must have been something else; namely, an understanding that theologically the four canonical gospels represented most closely the living faith of most people in the churches.

When we turn to the remainder of the New Testament, there is clear evidence of theological schools from which only certain books were selected as "genuine." The Pastoral Letters show one type of development in the Pauline school, whereas Hebrews would appear to represent something quite different but nevertheless bearing Paul's name. The letters of Peter and John show the existence of Petrine and Johannine theological schools. All of these and others can be documented as arising out of developing traditions in various sections of the geographically spreading Christian church.[13]

---

2. *Korintherbrief* (*Wissenschaftliche Monographien zum Alten und Neuen Testament*, Vol. 11; Neukirchen: Neukirchener Verlag, 1964).

[12] Koester, *op. cit.*, pp. 236–241.

[13] For a comprehensive, yet concise survey, see Koester, "Gnomai Diaforoi: The Origin and Nature of Diversification in the History of Early Christianity," *Harvard Theological Review*, Vol. 58.2 (July,

Certainly the Gnostic gospels represent one tradition cut off from the canon, as were also certain traditions that have been preserved only in Syriac and Georgian literature.

The living traditions from which the canonical literature was taken are clearly demonstrable for the New Testament, and must be postulated for the Old Testament where the various schools can be observed in the literature, but no extracanonical material survives except for the later "intertestamental" literature, greatly increased in amount now by the Qumran discoveries. The basic question is this: How does the luxuriant variety hold together? How have communities used it, variety and all, while regarding it as authoritative?

V

Canon, of course, means a measuring stick by which what is true and authoritative is separated from what is not. It seems probable that the idea of canon began in Israel's covenant renewal ceremonies, ultimately stemming from the Mosaic covenant. In them, after the recital of the divine benevolence, there was always the reading of the divine requirement, the authoritative word from the Lord to the people.

In this concept the first full doctrine of the canon was developed in Babylon and imposed on the fifth-century province of Yehud (Judah) as constitutional law by Ezra. On his return to Palestine there is reported a huge covenant renewal service during which the Torah of Moses was read, expounded, and accepted by the people as their "constitution" (Ezra 10; Neh. 8–10).[14] Inasmuch as it is

---

1965), pp. 279–318. Indeed this and the article of Koester on the four gospels referred to above (n. 9) seem to me to provide an excellent framework for devising a fresh and exciting way to teach an introductory course in the New Testament. To treat the subject historically and theologically out of the vast range of available material via the history of tradition approach would avoid the often boring and excessively literary emphasis which takes so much time with the details of the synoptic problem, etc.

[14] For exposition, see G. von Rad, *Studies in Deuteronomy (Studies*

agreed that this was the completed Pentaeuch, a clear canonical theory must be understood as making its first appearance at this point, the theory which has been dominant in Judaism through the centuries. The authortative core of the Old Testament is the first five books, and the authoritative element in those books is the law, conceived as revealed mainly to Moses. It is the Word of God, but the word is a legal word which is positive law encompassing the whole of life's activity.

There is thus a canon within the canon, an authoritative core which holds the rest of the literature in its variety around it. This appears to have been the method by which the canon has been used as such throughout the history of the western world. To be sure, the authoritative core which holds the rest of the literature around it, usually as its interpretative principle, has not been the same as the Torah in the Jewish canon, but nevertheless, it appears always to have existed.

The early Church obviously did not see Torah in the Old Testament as the most important authoritative element. Instead, the whole literature was read prophetically for the manner in which God had prepared the soil for history's normative event which is the life, death, and resurrection of Christ. Central in the emerging literature to become the New Testament was the passion story of Jesus, together with his words and acts and those of the Apostles, especially Paul, which were commentary on Christ's meaning for church and world. It is probable that the viewpoint expressed in the Apostles' Creed was centrally operative and expressive of the controlling canonical principle.

During the medieval age an incarnational theology seems to have been dominant. All before Christ was a foreshadowing of his advent, death, and resurrection. All that came after him was an extension of Christ, the bishops and clergy being in the succession of Christ's apostles. It is doubtful that one can speak of Biblical "history" in any sense in which we use the term. Instead, the Biblical events belong to a special divine history, a world of God and his interventions of a special character and for a special purpose.

in Biblical Theology, No. 9; London: SCM Press, and Naperville, Ill., Alec Allenson, 1953), pp. 13 ff.

The reformers rejected much of this viewpoint for a history, special though it was, which was nevertheless real and factual as is our own history. In other words, they recovered the Old Testament as a history of divine grace, as well as of judgment.[15] Luther, because of his own experience, tended to see Romans 7–8 as central in the canon and as the typical experience of all people of God. All are under the law which brings man to despair because of his violations of it and his inability to keep it. Then salvation as a gift of God by faith is offered. While the center of the whole is Christ, the law and gospel are nevertheless present in both Testaments. Later in the post-Reformation epoch, the Old Testament itself will be viewed as God's presentation of his law which leads man to despair, while the New Testament is God's offer of grace in Christ. Calvin, of course, tried to overcome this Lutheran view of the intractable opposition of law and gospel. His third use of the law saw the sacramental and political portions of Old Testament law as serving a temporal function in old Israel but having been fulfilled in Christ. On the other hand, the moral law of Israel was indeed authoritative for all Christians. Nevertheless, the center of the Old Testament was not simply the moral will of God, but God's salvation and revelation to Israel as his people among whom in the fullness of time Jesus Christ was sent.[16]

The canon within the canon can be observed with special clarity during the last century's Biblical criticism and during the first quarter of this century. Under the influence of philosophical idealism what was understood as centrally important was an evolving history in which increasingly noble ideas and ideals came to the fore out of a primitive background. The center of the canon, therefore, was considered to be the teaching of the prophets (social justice and ethical monotheism) and that of Jesus, particularly as the

[15] Esp. helpful to me at this point has been the Harvard dissertation by James Samuel Preus, *From Shadow to Promise: Old Testament Interpretation from Augustine to the Young Luther* (Cambridge: Harvard University Press, 1969).

[16] Calvin's commentaries, which are often more revealing than his formal *Institutes of the Christian Religion,* must surely be listed as among the greatest scholarly achievements in Scriptural exposition in *modern* times.

latter gave expression to the ideal of self-giving love. The meaning of the historical Jesus was seen in the simple ethical interpretation of his teaching, before the Divine Man theologizing was placed around him, especially by Paul. As regards the Old Testament alone Protestant scholars were joined by their Reform Jewish counterparts in seeing the center and climax in the explicit mono-theism and universalism of Second Isaiah (Chaps. 40–55).

Since I am not equipped as an Old Testament scholar to provide a serious discussion of the history of western theology with the canonical principle in mind which has been suggested, perhaps the illustrations provided above will serve to give substance to a fairly obvious point. It is impossible to consider the actual meaning of canon apart from a survey of the reigning theology of a given people at a given time. The canon within the Scripture will be those portions of the literature which are conceived best to express what the theology believed to be most important and relevant for its particular era. The remainder of the Bible will be partially ignored, partially reinterpreted in the light of a theology's central inter-pretative position, and partially held in tension with what was deemed of central importance.

To find how the Bible actually acts canonically at any given mo-ment, one should not go to formal discussions of the canon. The truth is to be found in actual usage, and here the current theology of the user provides the interpretative principle whereby the canon within the canon can be discerned.

The position here defended may seem excessively relativistic. Yet two factors need to be stressed. One is that the Bible has great variety because people saw things differently, and differing historical moments brought forth, and still bring forth, responses tailored to the situation, that were relevant to the particularity of the moment. This variety plus the constantly changing historical situation has a canonical limiting factor, however, in the formal canon as a given, discussed at the beginning of this chapter. It is doubtful, therefore, that people who take the Bible seriously in some manner as revelation are characterized by limitless free varia-tion in attitude and behavior. The formal canon as a historical given imposes certain limits, just as the Talmud has imposed its limits upon, and identity to, those people throughout the world who have accepted it.

VI

Our final question, then, is with regard to the truth and authority of the literature within the canon. We can do no better here at the end of this chapter and book than to refer again to H. Richard Niebuhr's *The Meaning of Revelation.*[17] The historical relativism which is implied by what is written in this and in the preceding chapter affirms simply that man "is not only in time but time is in man. Moreover, and more significantly, the time that is in man is not abstract but particular and concrete; it is not a general category of time but rather the time of a definite society with distinct language, economic and political relations, religious faith and social organization."[18] One who understands how all our experience is historically mediated is surely not required to "believe that nothing is mediated through history."[19] Theology "must begin in Christian history and with Christian history because it has no other choice; in this sense it is forced to begin with revelation, meaning by that word simply historic faith. . . ."

> When a theology that has been convinced of its historical relativism speaks of revelation it means not only that in religion, as in other affairs, men are historically conditioned but also that to the limited point of view of historic Christian faith a reality discloses itself which invites all the trust and devotion of finite, temporal men. Such a theology of revelation is objectively relativistic, proceeding with confidence in the independent reality of what is seen, though recognizing that its assertions about that reality are meaningful only to those who look upon it from the same standpoint.[20]

Niebuhr quotes Whitehead to the effect that "religions commit suicide when they find their inspiration in their dogmas. The in-

[17] See above, n. 2.
[18] *Ibid.*, p. 13.
[19] *Ibid.*, pp. 18–19.
[20] *Ibid.*, p. 22.

spiration of religion lies in the history of religion." Metaphysical systems cannot maintain a community's intellectual life nor can abstract systems of value. "Idealistic and realistic metaphysics, perfectionist and hedonistic ethics, have been poor substitutes for the New Testament, and churches which feed on such nourishment seem subject to spiritual rickets."[21]

A confessional view of Scripture, rather than a doctrinal, is the only theological stance in which its authority can be discerned. The Church has never meant that revelation simply means Scripture. It is rather a Scripture which becomes our history, read in a community in which men listen for the Word of God when it is read. Its truth is truth-for-us, or saving truth, heard by a community exhibiting a common trust in the Spirit, the Spirit of Truth, which alone can confirm it. "The Scriptures point to God and through Scriptures God points to men when they are read by those who share the same background which the community which produced the letter possessed, or by those who participate in the common life of which the Scriptures contain the record."[22] Niebuhr's book continues with discussions of revelation, not as history, but as in history, with imagination and reason, "reasons of the heart," and with the deity of God whom revelation reveals.

From an abstract viewpoint the problem of the Scripture's truth and validity cannot be solved. If the truth of the images of Scripture is sought, does one seek correspondence with some reality outside it? Yet the problem of the correspondence theory of truth "is that images can only be compared with images. They can never be compared with outside reality. The difficulty with the coherence theory of truth, on the other hand, is that coherence or consistency of the image is simply not what we mean by truth."[23] We can examine the consistency, coherence, survival value, stability, and organizing power in the Biblical manner of understanding God and ourselves in our world. Yet in the end we can never measure this

---

[21] *Ibid.*, p. 47.
[22] *Ibid.*, pp. 50–51.
[23] Kenneth E. Boulding, *The Image* (Ann Arbor Paperbooks, University of Michigan Press, 1961), p. 165. For the context of his discussion, see above, the first section of Chap. 6.

Biblical reality with Reality itself, whether we attempt the measurement in the field of value or in the field of fact. If we could do so, we should be able, far more than we are, to penetrate the merging point of symbol and reality. As regards the truth of the canonical Scripture, it would appear that we must settle for a much humbler quest than for absolute certainty in epistemology. It would be a quest for those factors of organization of experience which provide most meaning and most creativity, while they humble one before mystery we cannot penetrate. They can never be concrete tests of validity because God has not committed his truth to respond adequately to our tests.

Index

Abrahamic covenant, 138n., 116n.
acts of God, 33, 43, 46, 49, 51f., 80,
    109
adaptation to environment, 90ff.
Aharoni, Y,, 105n.
Albright, W. F., 74n., 102, 127n.
Alt, A., 108n.
Anderson, B. W., 30, 75n., 77n.,
    140n.
anthropology, biblical, 63ff., 80
apocalyptic, 141ff., 178
archaeology and the creative in his-
    tory, 84f., 95

Bach, J. S., 20
Bailyn, B., 99n.
Baltzer, K., 61f., 106n., 109n.
Barr, J., 46ff.
Barth, K., 19, 22f., 49
Bedouin ideal, 104n.
Bellah, R., 113n.
Blackman, E. C., 49n.
Boman, T., 45n.
Boulding, K. E., 151ff., 184n.
Bright, J., 109n., 174n.
Brown, R. E., 118n.
Brunner, E., 23n., 28n., 40ff.
Buber, M., 108n.
Bultmann, R., 10, 19, 30ff., 58,
    110n., 147n., 157f.
Burrill, D. R., 17n.
Burrow, M., 55

Calvin, J., 10, 20n., 25, 154ff., 160,
    165, 181
Campbell, B., 87n., 91n.
Campbell, E. F., 106n., 108n., 117n.,
    118
canonicity, 10f., 166ff., 179ff.
chaos, 71, 75f., 79

Childs, B. S., 55f.
Christian hymns and the Old Testa-
    ment, 33ff.
Christomonism, 13ff.
    in Barthian theology, 22 ff.
    in existentialist theology, 29ff.
    in pietism, 18ff.
Chronicler, 176
Clements, R. E., 75n., 77n., 125n.,
    138n.
Cobb, J. B., 50n., 68n., 147n.
confession, 27f., 43, 47, 184
Confession, United Presbyterian,
    24ff., 100
conflict in history, 93ff., 121, 148f.
Conquest theme, 123ff., 131ff.
Corbin, H., 44n.
cosmic government, 97f., 109f., 116,
    119, 121, 133, 147f.
cosmic mountain, 132n., 139n.
covenant
    Abrahamic, 116n., 138n.
    Book of the, 111
    centrality of, 57f., 61f.
    Davidic, 114n., 135, 137ff.
    love, 114f.
    Mosaic, 104ff., 138
    New Testament, 103, 116f.
    renewal, 28, 109, 111, 135
    vassal treaties, 104ff.
Cox, H., 166
creation
    and history, 81ff., 92f., 95
    in epic traditions, 77, 80
    in Israelite thought, 72ff., 80f., 95
    in polytheism, 71ff.
    in Psalms 104–106, 77f.
    in royal theology, 74f.
    in Second Isaiah, 78f.
    in wisdom, 75ff., 81

187

Crosby, F., 21
Cross, F. M., 70n., 102, 131, 133, 134f., 142n., 144n., 171ff.
Cutler, D. R., 113n.

Darwin, C., 85
David, 75, 81
Day of the Lord, 140
Dead Sea Scrolls, 19, 141f., 171ff.
"death of god," 18, 73
demythologizing of nature, 72f., 88
Descartes, R., 63
de Vaux, R., 53ff., 109n.
Deuteronomic Code, 111
Deuteronomic history, 47, 175
Deuteronomy, Book of, 175
Dirksen, E. M., 166
Dobzhansky, T., 88f.
Dowey, E. A., 25, 154n., 157, 160

Eichrodt, W., 39, 57ff., 66, 106n.
Eissfeldt, O., 55, 108n.
El, 70, 102
Elder, J. D., 113n.
election
   of Israel, 33, 79, 107, 109
   of David and Zion, 75
Eliade, M., 47, 72
Elliger, K., 105n.
epic tradition, 43, 174
event and revelation, 39ff., 164
evolution of man, 85ff.
   related to the creative, 88ff., 95
existence of God, 17f., 23
Existentialism, 15ff., 29f., 35ff., 63, 145f.
Exodus, 44, 81, 109, 134
   Second, 79, 95, 140, 142
Ezra, 76n., 111, 175f., 179

fatherhood of God, 101ff., 117f.
fatherhood names, 102f.
Feuerbach, L., 23
Filson, F., 105n.
Frankfort, H., 47, 72n.
Freedman, D. N., 131

Georgi, D., 177
Gerstenberger, E., 106n.
Gilgal, 134ff.

Glueck, N., 114n.
god of the fathers, 102f.
Golden, H., 122
Gospel hymns, 21f.
Gospel of Thomas, 177
Greek thought, 40, 45, 48, 72f.
graciousness of suzerain, 106, 108f., 113ff.
Gunkel, H., 48

Handel, G. F., 21
Haroutunian, J., 63f.
Haupt, P., 25
Hays, A. A., 157n.
"heaven" as seat of government, 97f.
Hegel, F., 16
Heidegger, M., 36, 146n.
Heinemann, 118n.
Heisenberg, W., 162f.
hesed, 75, 114n.
Hillers, D., 106n.
history and revelation, 10, 27, 32, 43f., 46ff., 57, 68f., 91, 183f.
Hittite treaty forms, 105f.
hôdāh, 28n.
Holiness Code, 111
holy war, 126ff.
Hooft, V. 't, 24n.
Huffmon, H. B., 102n., 115n.

Idealism, 121, 181f.

Jacobsen, T., 47, 72n., 102
James, W., 16f., 28, 36
Jenks, A. W., 174n.
Jeroboam I, 102
John, 14, 117f., 143
John of Damascus, 33
Jonas, H., 147n.
Joshua, Book of, 122ff.

Kant, I., 17n., 22f., 95n.
Kaufman, G. D., 63n., 67, 68, 82n., 92n.
Kerr, D. W., 28n.
kerygma and the Gospels, 176
Kierkegaard, S., 15f.
Kingdom of God, 18, 25, 117f., 165
Kingship of Yahweh, 108
kinship names, 102

knowledge, nature of, 151ff., 161ff.
knowledge of God, 109f., 154f.
Koester, H., 176ff.
Köhler, L., 97
Korosec, V., 106n.
Kraus, H.-J., 127n., 134n.

law and gospel, 110f., 181
Leakey, L. S. B., 86f.
local text types, 171ff.
Luther, M., 160, 181

McCarthy, D., 106n.
McKenzie, J., 31
Madison, J., 99f.
man, view of
  biblical, 63ff., 80
  historical vs. ontological, 91f.
Marcionism, 100
Margenau, H., 161f.
Masoretic text, 170ff.
Meland, B. E., 82n., 95
melek, 74, 108
Mendenhall, G. E., 61f., 104ff.
Messiah, 13f., 28f., 31
Miles, C. A., 22
miracle stories, 177f.
monarchy in Israel, 74f.
monotheism, 107f.
Moran, W. L., 114f.
Mosaic covenant, 104ff., 138
Mowinckel, S., 43n., 80n., 140n.
Muilenburg, J., 106n.
Myer, E., 90, 91n.
myth and history, 47f., 80f., 133f.
mythical language, 79, 131ff., 137f.

nāqām, 114n.
New Testament, relation to Old,
  30ff., 59, 100f., 116ff., 121,
  141ff.
Niebuhr, H. Richard, 9, 20n., 26,
  168, 183f.
Niebuhr, Reinhold, 81, 145n., 146
Noth, M., 43n., 47, 109n., 174f.

Old Testament
  and Christology, 13f., 28, 37f.
  in Christian hymns, 33ff.
  theology, 39ff., 50ff., 68f.

Orlinsky, H. M., 127n., 170
orthogenesis, 90, 92

Pannenberg, W., 49, 50n., 68
Paul, 28f., 103, 111, 116, 124, 143,
  182
Pedersen, J., 104, 131n.
Pentateuch, 76, 111, 176, 180
pietism, 19f.
political terminology, 10, 18f., 24f.,
  107, 112f., 133f., 144ff., 164f.
  objections to, 99f., 110, 119
polytheism, nature of, 71f.
Preus, J. S., 181n.
process theology, 82ff., 95
promised land, 105
prophets, role of, 52, 74
Proto-Lucianic text, 171
Proto-Theodotionic text, 172

Q-source, 177

Revelation, Book of, 143f.
revelation and Christ, 23ff., 34f.
revelation and history, 10, 27, 32,
  43f., 46ff., 57, 68f., 91, 183f.
revelation as event, 39ff., 164
Riemann, P., 104n.
ritual, function in polytheism, 71f.
Robinson, H. W., 64n.
Robinson, J. A. T., 64n.
Robinson, J. M., 50n., 68n., 147n.
royal liturgy, 135ff.
royal theology, 74f.
Rudolph, W., 174n.
Rylaardsdam, J. C., 76n.

Samuel, 74
Sanders, J. A., 173n.
Schniewind, J., 176
secularization, 112
Simpson, G. G., 90, 91n., 92n.
Sinai tradition, 61f., 109
Smith, W. C., 56n.
social reform, biblical roots, 112f.
Stekelis, M., 87
Stendahl, K., 142n.
Stephen, 125
suzerainty treaty, 105ff.

symbol, 158ff.
Synoptic Gospels, 142

Tanis, J. R., 20n.
Tax, S., 86n.
Teilhard de Chardin, 86, 89f.
Tertullian, 100f.
Tetrateuch, 174f.
textual criticism, 169ff.
theology, nature of, 9, 52, 54ff., 61ff., 66f.
theophoric names, 14, 102f.
Thomas Aquinas, 154
Tillich, P., 10, 17n., 116, 148ff., 158n., 165
tôdāh, 28n.
Torrance, T. F., 156ff.
tribal league, 74, 81, 109, 111, 127f.
Trinity, 13, 25f., 38
Trotter, F. T., 73
Trueblood, E., 13, 18n., 24

uncertainty in physics, 161ff.
United Presbyterian Confession, 24ff., 100

vassal treaty, 105ff.
Voegelin, E., 48, 58n.

Volz, P., 174n.
von Rad, G., 39, 42f., 47, 50ff., 65f., 68, 77n., 79, 109n., 127n., 128n., 140n., 174n., 179n.
Vriezen, T. C., 55

Wieman, N., 82f., 93, 95
Wilder, A., 28
Wilder, T., 94
Williams, D. D., 98f.
Williams, G. H., 34n.
Willis, E. D., 158n.
Wilson, E., 19
Wilson, J., 72n.
Whitehead, A. N., 82, 95, 98, 110, 119, 149, 183
word of God, 25, 32, 74, 76f.
work as vocation, 112
World Council of Churches, 23
Wright, G. E., 11, 42, 46n., 61, 64n., 74n., 77n., 101n., 104n., 105n., 106n., 107n., 109n., 127n.

yāda', 115n.

Zimmerli, W., 28n.
Zwingli, U., 160

Format by Ellen Brecher
Set in Times Roman
Composed and printed by York Composition Company, Inc.
Bound by The Haddon Craftsmen, Inc.
HARPER & ROW, PUBLISHERS, INCORPORATED